Awaken Your Consciousness: Essence Evolution

Table of Contents

Part 1: Foundations of Awakening
Chapter 1: Understanding Consciousness Awakening
Chapter 2: The Essence of Spiritual Awakening
Chapter 3: 3D Reality: The Physical World and Its Attachments
Chapter 4: 4D Consciousness: The Transition Phase
Chapter 5: 5D Consciousness: A New Paradigm

Part 2: Inner Transformation and Healing
Chapter 6: Ego vs. Spiritual Self: Recognizing the Inner Battle
Chapter 7: Letting Go of 3D Attachments
Chapter 10: Inner Child Healing: Reconnecting with Your Authentic Self
Chapter 9: Shadow Integration: Embracing the Hidden Parts of You
Chapter 8: Healing and Integration: Mind, Body, and Spirit
Chapter 11: Integration of Past Lives and Karma: Healing Across Timelines

Part 3: Practices for Evolving Consciousness
Chapter 12: Raising Your Vibration: Becoming a Magnetic Force for Good
Chapter 13: Understanding Mindfulness: The Foundation of Awareness
Chapter 14: Sound and Vibration: Frequencies for Healing and Transformation
Chapter 15: Connecting with Nature: Reclaiming Your Natural Wisdom
Chapter 16: Spiritual Practices for 5D Living
Chapter 17: Living in 5D: Transforming Relationships, Career, and Daily Life

Table of Contents

Part 3 Continued
Chapter 18: Awakening Through Relationships
Chapter 19: Sacred Feminine and Masculine Integration
Chapter 20: Energy Healing Modalities

Part 4: Advanced Exploration of Consciousness
Chapter 21: Intuition and Psychic Development: Accessing Higher Knowledge
Chapter 22: Kundalini Awakening: Unlocking the Energy Within
Chapter 23: Quantum Consciousness: Exploring Infinite Possibilities
Chapter 24: Manifesting and Co-Creation: Designing Your Reality
Chapter 25: Advanced Practices for Deepening Consciousness

Part 5: Collective and Cosmic Evolution
Chapter 26: The Collective Shift: How Your Evolution Contributes to Humanity's Awakening
Chapter 27: Living in Alignment: Continuing the Journey of Evolution
Chapter 28: Unity of One Consciousness: Embracing Interconnectedness
Chapter 29: Involution: Turning Inward for True Growth

Conclusion: Embracing the Journey of Awakening

Final Thoughts

'ZEN' REPRESENTS A VOICE OF REFLECTION AND INSIGHT WOVEN THROUGHOUT THIS BOOK TO INSPIRE DEEPER CONTEMPLATION.

I dedicate this book to you, the reader.
As someone who has walked the path of self-discovery and continues to progress toward deeper consciousness, I understand the challenges, triumphs, and moments of profound insight that accompany this journey. This book is a culmination of my awareness, insights, and practices, shared in the hope that they will serve as a beacon of light on your unique path.

I hope that at least some part of this book provides you with the assistance, inspiration, or comfort you need to grow in the direction your personal journey requires. Whether you find solace in mindfulness practices, healing in sacred sounds, or awakening in connection with nature, know that each step in your growth is valuable and perfect in its own way.

If you are reading this, trust that your higher self has guided you to this book. Trust in that guidance, and allow it to lead you toward deeper understanding, greater compassion for yourself and others, and a profound sense of awakening.

May this book be a companion on your journey, offering support and suggestions as you navigate the process of consciousness. Embrace your unique essence, trust in your inner wisdom, and let your light shine brightly.

Love & Light,
K. Martin

Understanding Essence Evolution

Essence Evolution is about supporting and encouraging everyone's unique and individual consciousness awakening journey. The term itself signifies the unfolding and blossoming of our true selves, transcending beyond the limitations of the ego and societal conditioning. It is an ongoing process of becoming more aligned with our natural, higher selves, embracing the lessons life offers, and breaking free from cycles of karma.

My Journey to Essence Evolution

My own journey has been filled with experiences that led me to realize I was often living from my ego, victim mentality, self. I was completely disconnected from my true essence. Through various trials and reflections, I came to understand that I am a spiritual being having a human experience. I realized that I am not my mind. My mind was running on 40 years of programming that I was not consciously aware of. My mind was in control of me and it was time to take my power back. This realization allowed me to see my experiences as lessons, opportunities for growth and transformation, rather than as barriers.

By embracing the lessons from these experiences, I began to break my patterns and cycles. I believe we are all here to grow into our natural spiritual selves. This process happens uniquely for each individual, shaped by their experiences and perspectives and in their own timeframe.

The Purpose of This Book

The purpose of this book is to inspire others to be comfortable with doing what they need for themselves throughout their awakening journey. It's a call to recognize that everyone's path is different, and that is where the beauty lies. Whether you are just starting or have been on this path for some time, this book aims to offer gentle love and support. It aims to offer ideas that may help you on your journey. Use what makes you feel good.

We live in a society that often pressures us to conform and fit into predefined boxes. However, true awakening comes from embracing our differences and being authentically ourselves. This book encourages you to lovingly embrace your uniqueness and to grow in alignment with your higher self. You were not made to "fit in" so stop trying!

Embracing the Present Moment

A fundamental aspect of Essence Evolution is the understanding that we are all exactly where we need to be at this very moment. Regardless of how negative a situation may seem, it is happening FOR us, not to us. Everything stems from us internally, nothing is external. The external is a mirror of what we express internally. Listen to your thoughts. Practice becoming aware of when your mind is in control and when you are in control of your mind. Every experience is an opportunity for growth and learning. By embracing and being grateful for the present moment, we can begin to see the perfection in our journey.

By being present we also learn to pay attention to our thoughts. We learn to recognize the programming we have and to analyze if that is a believe we want to continue to have or not. We can choose to create a new program. Delete the old program and decide what YOU want to believe. Become conscious and awaken!

Encouragement for Your Journey
This book is designed to be a companion on your journey, offering insights, practices, and reflections that can help you connect more deeply with your true self. I encourage you to take and use what resonates with you, and to leave what doesn't. Your journey is your own, and there is no one right way to awaken.

Remember that you are a unique and perfect expression of the divine. Embrace your journey with love, compassion, and authenticity. Trust that you are exactly where you need to be, and that every step you take is leading you closer to your true self.

Welcome to the journey of Essence Evolution. May it bring you inspiration, growth, and a deeper connection to your authentic self.

In the context of spiritual awakening, 3D, 4D, and 5D refer to different levels of consciousness, perception, and experience rather than physical dimensions. These concepts help us understand how our awareness and interaction with reality can evolve as we grow spiritually and emotionally.

3D (Third Dimension): This is the level of consciousness where most of humanity resides. It is deeply rooted in the physical world and duality—right vs. wrong, good vs. bad. At this level, people often perceive life through the lens of materialism, survival, and separation. The focus is on external circumstances, linear time, and tangible experiences.

4D (Fourth Dimension): The 4D is a transitional state of consciousness, a bridge between the physical and the spiritual. In this dimension, awareness begins to expand beyond the material. It is characterized by a greater understanding of interconnectedness, emotional healing, and the concept of co-creation. Time feels more fluid, and people start to question limiting beliefs and embrace higher perspectives.

5D (Fifth Dimension): The 5D is the state of unity consciousness, unconditional love, and living in alignment with the soul's purpose. In this dimension, duality dissolves, and individuals experience a profound sense of oneness with all life. The focus shifts to compassion, intuitive guidance, and living authentically in harmony with universal energy. These dimensions are not places but states of being that reflect our level of awareness and vibration. The journey from 3D to 5D is deeply personal, often involving inner work, healing, and a commitment to growth. Embracing this journey allows us to align with our higher selves and experience life with greater peace, purpose, and connection.

Essence Evolution: Awaken Your Consciousness

Introduction: The Journey to Awakening

We live in an extraordinary time—a time where more people are beginning to awaken to the deeper truths of existence, and where the pursuit of higher consciousness is no longer a journey for a few but for the many. The world as we know it, with its constant demands for material success, power, and control, has begun to lose its appeal. Many of us sense that there is something more, something beyond the tangible, something that calls us toward a reality based not on fear and separation, but on love, unity, and inner peace. This journey is the essence of what is often referred to as the shift into 5D consciousness—a state where you align with the frequency of love, compassion, and your higher self. To understand what it means to live in 5D, we must first explore where most of us have been for much of our lives: in 3D consciousness. In 3D, we are ruled by ego, survival, and the external world's demands. The 3D world is one of competition, scarcity, and fear—a reality that many are seeking to transcend.

Moving from 3D to 5D is a journey of the soul, an evolution of your essence, a return to your authentic self. It is the process of rediscovering who you truly are and letting go of the limitations and fears that have held

you back. This book will guide you through that transformation. Whether you're just beginning your awakening journey or have already experienced glimpses of higher consciousness, the insights and practices shared here will help you evolve into a more aligned, expansive, and joyful version of yourself.
In 5D, you live from the heart. You begin to see yourself as an integral part of the whole—connected to others, nature, and the universe in profound ways. Life flows more easily as you embrace your true nature and live in harmony with the energetic forces that govern our world. You start to co-create your reality, empowered by love, intuition, and a deeper understanding of your purpose. This is the power of evolving your essence.
The world is awakening, and you are a part of this grand evolution. As more people shift into 5D consciousness, the collective consciousness of humanity rises, allowing for a reality where peace, love, and unity become the norm. This is not just an individual journey—it is a global one.

Join me in exploring the path to higher consciousness, where the limitations of the past are left behind, and the boundless possibilities of the future unfold.

Part 1

FOUNDATIONS OF AWAKENING

chapter 1

UNDERSTANDING THE DIMENSIONS OF CONSCIOUSNESS

"CONSCIOUSNESS IS NOT JUST A STATE OF BEING AWAKE; IT IS THE AWARENESS OF THE INFINITE LAYERS WITHIN YOURSELF AND THE UNIVERSE AROUND YOU."
– ZEN

Consciousness exists on a spectrum, encompassing different levels of awareness that shape our perception of reality and influence how we engage with the world. Each dimension represents a distinct state of being, with its own set of beliefs, behaviors, and experiences. The journey of spiritual growth often involves shifting through these dimensions, moving from the limitations of the physical and ego-driven 3D realm to the expansive, love-centered realm of 5D consciousness.

At the core of 3D consciousness is the focus on the material world. It is a dimension where individuals are primarily concerned with physical survival, personal achievements, and external validation. Life in this state often feels like a constant race, driven by the need for success, wealth, and social status. The ego plays a central role, shaping thoughts, behaviors, and relationships. The ego's voice echoes with demands for power, control, and superiority, perpetuating a sense of separation from others. This separation is reinforced by dualistic thinking, where life is viewed in stark contrasts —good versus bad, success versus failure, abundance versus scarcity. Within this paradigm, fear acts as the primary motivator, compelling individuals to seek security through material gains and to protect their sense of self from perceived threats.

However, the limitations of 3D consciousness eventually become apparent. Many people begin to feel that something is missing, that life is more than just accumulating wealth or achieving status. This is often the point where the shift to 4D consciousness begins.

The 4D realm serves as a bridge between the physical and the spiritual, a phase marked by increased awareness and a desire for deeper meaning. Individuals in 4D start to question societal norms, conditioned beliefs, and the pursuit of external success. Curiosity becomes a driving force, leading to the exploration of spiritual practices like meditation, energy healing, and mindfulness. It is here that people begin to sense a greater reality beyond the physical, experiencing synchronicities, intuitive nudges, and moments of profound insight.

Healing is a central theme in 4D consciousness. As people expand their awareness, suppressed emotions, unresolved traumas, and limiting beliefs surface for integration. This can be both liberating and challenging, as it requires facing aspects of the self that were previously ignored or denied. Shadow work, the process of embracing and integrating these hidden parts of the self, becomes essential for personal growth. The practice of inner child healing also emerges, as individuals reconnect with wounded aspects from childhood that have shaped their behaviors and beliefs.

Moving into 5D consciousness is a transformative leap into a heart-centered way of living. Here, life is guided by love, compassion, and a sense of unity with all beings. In 5D, the perception of duality dissolves, replaced by a deep understanding that everything is interconnected. Individuals experience a profound sense of oneness, where separation is an illusion and all actions are seen as contributing to the collective whole.

This dimension emphasizes co-creation, where individuals recognize that their thoughts, intentions, and energy shape their reality. Manifestation becomes more fluid and effortless, as people align with their higher selves and the flow of the universe.

The transition from 3D to 5D is not a linear path but a spiral of growth, often involving moments of regression and breakthrough. It requires a willingness to let go of old beliefs, heal emotional wounds, and embrace a higher perspective. The journey can be daunting, as it involves facing the ego's fears, releasing attachments, and learning to trust the inner guidance of the heart. Yet, it is also profoundly rewarding, offering a life of greater peace, joy, and alignment with the soul's purpose.

As you embark on this journey of expanding consciousness, it is important to approach it with an open heart and a sense of curiosity. Each dimension offers unique lessons and opportunities for growth, inviting you to explore new facets of yourself and the universe. The shift from 3D to 5D is not just an individual process but part of a collective awakening, where each person's evolution contributes to the global shift toward unity and love.

QUESTIONS FOR CONTEMPLATION

Take a moment to reflect on the following questions for contemplation. You can think about your answers, jot them down on the "notes" page provided in this book, in a notebook, or explore them more deeply in the companion workbook designed to complement this book (to be released early 2025).

Which dimension of consciousness do you feel most connected to right now, and why?

What beliefs or patterns have kept you rooted in 3D thinking, and how can you begin to shift them toward a higher perspective?

How do you currently experience synchronicities or intuitive guidance? Are you open to seeing them as signs of alignment with 4D or 5D consciousness?

What does living from the heart mean to you, and what steps can you take to embody more love, compassion, and unity in your daily life?

NOTES

chapter 2

THE ESSENCE OF SPIRITUAL AWAKENING

"SPIRITUAL AWAKENING IS NOT ABOUT BECOMING SOMETHING NEW; IT IS ABOUT REMEMBERING WHO YOU HAVE ALWAYS BEEN." – ZEN

The Stages of Awakening

Awakening is a deeply personal yet universal journey, often unfolding through distinct stages of awareness and transformation. It begins with a sense of discontent or curiosity—an inner stirring that challenges the status quo of life in the physical, or 3D, reality. In this stage, individuals often feel drawn to question societal norms, material attachments, and conditioned beliefs. As this questioning deepens, the transition to 4D consciousness emerges, where expanded awareness begins to take root. Here, a shift occurs from external validation to inner exploration, and the interconnectedness of all things becomes clearer. It's a space of profound self-discovery, but also one of challenges, as old patterns and limiting beliefs surface for release.

The journey continues toward 5D consciousness, a state of being that transcends duality and embraces unity, love, and higher vibrational living. In this stage, life becomes less about striving and more about aligning—living with purpose, authenticity, and harmony. Each stage of awakening offers unique lessons and opportunities for growth, with no definitive timeline or endpoint. It is a spiraling process, inviting individuals to deepen their awareness, heal, and expand continuously. These stages are not rigid; they are fluid and cyclical, reflecting the dynamic nature of spiritual evolution. Together, they guide us toward embodying our highest essence and contributing to the collective awakening of humanity.

We live in an extraordinary time—a time where more people are beginning to awaken to the deeper truths of existence, and where the pursuit of higher consciousness is no longer a journey for a few but for the many. The world as we know it, with its constant demands for material success, power, and control, has begun to lose its appeal. Many of us sense that there is something more, something beyond the tangible, something that calls us toward a reality based not on fear and separation, but on love, unity, and inner peace. This journey is the essence of what is often referred to as the shift into 5D consciousness—a state where you align with the frequency of love, compassion, and your higher self. To understand what it means to live in 5D, we must first explore where most of us have been for much of our lives: in 3D consciousness. In 3D, we are ruled by ego, survival, and the external world's demands. The 3D world is one of competition, scarcity, and fear—a reality that many are seeking to transcend.

Moving from 3D to 5D is a journey of the soul, an evolution of your essence, a return to your authentic self. It is the process of rediscovering who you truly are and letting go of the limitations and fears that have held you back. This book will guide you through that transformation. Whether you're just beginning your awakening journey or have already experienced glimpses of higher consciousness, the insights and practices shared here will help you evolve into a more aligned, expansive, and joyful version of yourself.

In 5D, you live from the heart. You begin to see yourself as an integral part of the whole—connected to others, nature, and the universe in profound ways. Life flows more easily as you embrace your true nature and live in harmony with the energetic forces that govern our world. You start to co-create your reality, empowered by love, intuition, and a deeper understanding of your purpose. This is the power of evolving your essence. The world is awakening, and you are a part of this grand evolution. As more people shift into 5D consciousness, the collective consciousness of humanity rises, allowing for a reality where peace, love, and unity become the norm. This is not just an individual journey—it is a global one.

Affirmations for Awakening

I am open to the infinite possibilities of awakening my true self.

With each breath, I align with my higher consciousness and inner truth.

I trust the journey of self-discovery and embrace the lessons it brings.

The light of awareness within me grows stronger every day.

I honor the unfolding of my unique awakening, knowing I am exactly where I need to be.

chapter 3

3D CONSCIOUSNESS - THE PHYSICAL REALITY & ITS ATTACHMENTS

"THE PHYSICAL REALITY WE PERCEIVE IS BUT A SHADOW OF A DEEPER TRUTH, SHAPED BY OUR BELIEFS, ACTIONS, AND PERCEPTIONS."
– ZEN

3D consciousness is rooted in the physical realm, where life is governed by the tangible and the measurable. In this state, the ego thrives, driving individuals to seek validation, security, and success through material achievements. The pursuit of wealth, status, and recognition becomes the primary focus, often overshadowing deeper spiritual needs. The ego operates from a place of fear, compelling individuals to protect their sense of self through comparison, competition, and control. It's a dimension where life feels like a constant struggle—an endless pursuit of "more," whether it's more money, more possessions, or more approval.

The nature of 3D consciousness is fundamentally dualistic, defined by rigid categories of right and wrong, good and bad, success and failure. This black-and-white thinking reinforces a sense of separation, both within oneself and between individuals. Relationships are often transactional, based on what can be gained rather than genuine connection. This creates a cycle of disconnection, where even moments of achievement feel fleeting, leaving a sense of emptiness and unfulfillment. The scarcity mindset dominates, leading people to believe that there isn't enough to go around. This mindset fuels behaviors like hoarding resources, competing relentlessly, and fearing the loss of what has been acquired.

As individuals begin to feel the limitations of this dimension, they often encounter a deep sense of dissatisfaction. Despite accumulating possessions or achieving status, there remains a nagging feeling that something essential is missing.

This dissatisfaction serves as a catalyst for change, prompting the individual to question the assumptions and beliefs that have driven them thus far. It is the first sign of awakening, a crack in the armor of the ego that allows for a glimpse of something greater.

The journey beyond 3D consciousness starts with awareness—recognizing the patterns of thought and behavior that are rooted in fear, control, and separation. This recognition is often accompanied by discomfort, as it requires facing the aspects of oneself that have been driven by ego rather than the heart. It is a humbling process, one that asks for honesty, vulnerability, and a willingness to release the attachments that no longer serve growth.

Breaking free from 3D consciousness is not about abandoning the physical world but redefining one's relationship with it. It involves shifting from a focus on accumulation to a focus on alignment, where success is no longer measured by what is owned but by how aligned one is with their true values and purpose. The scarcity mindset is replaced by an abundance mindset, where individuals start to believe in the possibility of limitless opportunities, love, and fulfillment. Relationships also transform, moving from transactions to genuine connections based on mutual growth, respect, and understanding.

In this process, the ego does not disappear, but its grip loosens. The desire for control gives way to trust in the flow of life, where outcomes are not forced but allowed to unfold naturally.

The sense of competition dissolves, replaced by a sense of collaboration and unity. The journey beyond 3D consciousness is one of remembering—a return to the heart, where love, compassion, and inner peace become the guiding forces of life.

In many ways, 3D consciousness is about separation. We feel separated from others, from nature, and even from our own higher selves. We define our worth by external markers—how much money we have, how successful we are in our careers, how much material wealth we can accumulate. In the 3D world, fear is a powerful motivator, driving many of our decisions. We fear not having enough, not being enough, and not achieving enough.

Ego, Fear, and Survival

In 3D, the ego reigns supreme. It's the voice inside your head that constantly compares you to others, worries about the future, and holds onto past grievances. The ego is designed to protect us, but in 3D consciousness, it often becomes overactive, keeping us in a perpetual state of fear and survival mode.

We may think we are in control, but the truth is that fear controls us. We fear failure, rejection, and uncertainty. We live in a state of anxiety, constantly worrying about what others think of us or whether we are living up to society's expectations. Our ego tells us that we must constantly strive for more—more success, more possessions, more validation—to be happy.

But no matter how much we achieve in the 3D world, it never seems to be enough. The more we get, the more we want, and the cycle of dissatisfaction continues. This is the nature of 3D consciousness: it traps us in a loop of endless seeking, never fully satisfied, always looking outside of ourselves for fulfillment.

Separation and Duality

Another hallmark of 3D consciousness is separation. We see ourselves as separate from others, leading to feelings of isolation, competition, and judgment. This separation creates duality—the idea that life is divided into opposites: success vs. failure, right vs. wrong, good vs. evil. In 3D, we believe that we must take sides, that there is always an "us" vs. "them."

This duality creates conflict both within and outside of ourselves. We judge others for their differences, and we judge ourselves for not measuring up to the expectations set by society. We may even internalize these judgments, creating limiting beliefs about what we can achieve and what we deserve in life.

In the 3D world, scarcity is a common mindset. We believe that there is not enough—whether it's money, time, love, or success. This belief in scarcity leads to competition and a fear of loss. We believe that if someone else wins, we must lose, and so we hold tightly to what we have, afraid that it could be taken away at any moment.

The Role of the Physical

In 3D consciousness, the physical world is the ultimate reality. We focus on the tangible—what we can see, touch, and measure. Success is often defined by material possessions, status, and achievements. We become so absorbed in the external world that we lose sight of our inner world. The deeper spiritual truths of life are often ignored or dismissed as unimportant.

This focus on the external leads to a disconnection from our inner selves and from the higher aspects of consciousness. We may feel unfulfilled, even after achieving everything society tells us we need to be happy. This is because 3D consciousness is rooted in the belief that happiness comes from external circumstances, rather than from within.

Breaking Free from 3D Consciousness

While 3D consciousness may seem limiting, it is not inherently bad. It serves a purpose in our growth and evolution. The challenges of living in 3D—fear, ego, separation—are all opportunities for us to awaken to something greater. These challenges push us to seek more meaningful connections, question our beliefs, and ultimately evolve beyond the limitations of the 3D world.

Breaking free from 3D consciousness requires a shift in perspective. We must begin to question the reality we have been taught to accept and look within ourselves for answers. This is the first step toward awakening to 4D and 5D consciousness.

To start this process, we can:
- Recognize the patterns of fear, scarcity, and separation in our lives.
- Observe the ego without judgment, acknowledging when it tries to control our thoughts and actions.
- Question our beliefs about success, happiness, and self-worth, and whether they are based on external validation or inner truth.

By becoming aware of these 3D patterns, we create space for something new to emerge. We begin to see beyond the illusions of the 3D world and open ourselves to the higher realities of 4D and 5D consciousness.

"THE JOURNEY TO AWAKENING BEGINS WITH A SINGLE BREATH OF AWARENESS." – ZEN

Affirmations
to Embrace Awakening

"I release fear, judgment, and attachment, stepping fully into my higher truth."

"I am awakening to the limitless possibilities of my soul and the infinite wisdom within me."

"I choose love, compassion, and unity as I transcend the illusions of 3D reality."

"Every moment is a step toward my higher consciousness and spiritual alignment."

"I trust the process of awakening and embrace the journey with courage and gratitude."

QUESTIONS FOR CONTEMPLATION

How have you defined success up to this point in your life? Are these definitions aligned with your true values, or are they driven by external expectations?

In what ways has fear influenced your decisions, relationships, or career choices? How can you begin to choose love and alignment over fear?

Reflect on a recent moment when you felt compelled to compete or compare yourself to others. What underlying beliefs fueled this behavior, and how can you shift toward collaboration and connection?

What aspects of your current life bring genuine fulfillment, beyond material achievements? How can you nurture these aspects more deeply?

Notes

chapter 4

4D CONSCIOUSNESS - THE TRANSITION PHRASE

"THE BRIDGE BETWEEN DIMENSIONS IS BUILT WITH AWARENESS, WHERE THE MIND BEGINS TO SEE BEYOND THE LIMITS OF TIME AND SPACE."
— ZEN

The shift from 3D to 4D consciousness is a pivotal moment in the journey of awakening. It is a phase marked by a profound desire for deeper understanding, personal growth, and spiritual exploration. In 4D, individuals begin to question the established norms and beliefs that have governed their lives in the physical realm. This transition is not simply a change of mindset but a transformation of awareness, as individuals become attuned to subtler realities beyond the physical. At the core of 4D consciousness is the expansion of awareness. Life becomes less about external achievements and more about inner exploration. People find themselves drawn to spiritual practices, seeking answers to questions that cannot be satisfied by material success alone. Meditation, energy healing, breathwork, and other modalities become gateways to a more profound sense of self and reality. In this dimension, synchronicities start to appear frequently, often acting as guideposts that confirm one's alignment with the spiritual path. These meaningful coincidences are seen not as random occurrences but as messages from the universe, guiding individuals toward their higher purpose.

The 4D phase is also characterized by increased sensitivity, both emotionally and energetically. As individuals become more aware of the energies around them, they often experience heightened empathy, sometimes feeling overwhelmed by others' emotions or the collective energy of the environment.

This can be both a gift and a challenge, as it requires learning how to manage energy, set boundaries, and cleanse the aura regularly. The emotional landscape of 4D consciousness is often turbulent, as suppressed feelings, unresolved traumas, and limiting beliefs surface for healing. This process, known as shadow work, involves facing the darker, hidden parts of the self that have been repressed or denied.

Shadow work is one of the most transformative aspects of 4D consciousness. It requires courage, honesty, and a willingness to embrace vulnerability. As individuals confront their shadows, they discover aspects of themselves that hold immense power and wisdom. The integration of these shadow aspects leads to greater authenticity, wholeness, and self-acceptance. Inner child healing is another crucial component of this dimension, as it addresses wounds from childhood that continue to influence adult behavior and beliefs. Reconnecting with the inner child is both healing and liberating, allowing individuals to release patterns of fear, shame, or unworthiness that originated in early life.

Intuition also becomes stronger in 4D consciousness, serving as a bridge between the mind and the higher self. Individuals start to trust their inner voice more, recognizing it as a source of wisdom and guidance. This intuitive awakening is often accompanied by a growing interest in psychic phenomena, such as clairvoyance, telepathy, or receiving messages through dreams.

As people deepen their connection to their intuitive abilities, they learn to navigate life with greater ease, making decisions that align with their soul's purpose. Despite the beauty and growth associated with 4D consciousness, it can also be a challenging phase. Many individuals experience what is known as the "dark night of the soul," a period of intense inner struggle, confusion, and existential questioning. This dark night is often a necessary part of the spiritual journey, as it strips away false identities, beliefs, and attachments, paving the way for a more authentic and fulfilling existence. It is a phase that tests resilience, demanding surrender, trust, and faith in the process of transformation.

The transition to 4D consciousness is not always linear. People often fluctuate between 3D and 4D, revisiting old patterns as new layers of healing emerge. This back-and-forth movement is a normal part of spiritual growth, as each step forward involves deeper integration of past experiences and lessons. The key to navigating this dimension is to remain open, curious, and compassionate with oneself. It is not about reaching perfection but embracing progress, however gradual it may be.

Awakening and Self-Discovery

The hallmark of 4D consciousness is the process of awakening. You start to awaken to the realization that there is more to life than what you can see or measure. You begin to understand that your thoughts and emotions have a direct impact on your reality. This is a time of self-discovery, where you start to explore your inner world and ask profound questions:

- Who am I beyond my ego and my material success?
- What is my purpose here?
- What is the nature of reality?

This phase can feel liberating, as you begin to shed old identities and beliefs that no longer serve you. You might discover new passions, spiritual practices, or healing modalities that resonate with the deeper part of your soul. You may also begin to see the interconnectedness of all things, realizing that you are not separate from others or from the universe.

Releasing Limiting Beliefs

In 4D consciousness, a significant part of the journey is about releasing limiting beliefs that have kept you stuck in 3D thinking. These beliefs often stem from fear, scarcity, and a sense of unworthiness, which were reinforced by the ego. As you become more aware of these limiting beliefs, you can begin the process of letting them go and replacing them with new, empowering ones.

For example, you may have grown up believing that you need to work hard to be successful, or that you're not good enough unless you achieve a certain level of status or wealth. In 4D consciousness, you start to question these beliefs and recognize that your worth is inherent, not tied to external validation.

This process of letting go can be uncomfortable, as it requires facing the fears and insecurities that have been buried within you. However, it is through this healing process that you begin to free yourself from the chains of the past and step into a more authentic version of yourself.

Healing and Shadow Work

One of the most important aspects of 4D consciousness is healing. As you awaken to a new way of being, old wounds and traumas that you may have suppressed in the 3D world start to come to the surface. This is a natural part of the evolution process, as you can't fully move into higher states of consciousness without addressing and healing these aspects of yourself.

This phase often involves shadow work—the process of bringing the unconscious parts of yourself (your shadow) into the light of awareness. The shadow represents the parts of yourself that you've rejected, ignored, or judged, often because they were deemed unacceptable by society or by your own ego.

In 4D consciousness, you are called to confront and integrate these shadow aspects. This might involve working through feelings of shame, guilt, anger, or fear that have been repressed. Through this process, you come to understand that the shadow is not something to be feared but something to be embraced and healed.

Some key practices for healing and shadow work include:

- Journaling: Writing about your feelings, experiences, and memories can help bring unconscious thoughts and emotions to the surface.
- Meditation and Mindfulness: These practices allow you to observe your thoughts and emotions without judgment, helping you become more aware of patterns that need healing.
- Inner Child Work: Connecting with your inner child can help heal wounds from childhood that continue to affect your beliefs and behavior today.

Embracing the Flow of Life

As you evolve into 4D consciousness, you start to surrender to the flow of life. In 3D, there is a constant need to control, plan, and achieve. But in 4D, you begin to realize that the universe has a natural flow, and that by aligning with it, life becomes more harmonious. Instead of trying to force outcomes, you learn to trust the process and follow your intuition.

This doesn't mean you give up on your goals or desires—it simply means you stop resisting what is and allow things to unfold as they are meant to. This shift from resistance to acceptance is a key step in your evolution. As you let go of the need to control, you create space for new opportunities, relationships, and experiences to flow into your life.

Experiencing Synchronicities

A common experience in 4D consciousness is the appearance of synchronicities—meaningful coincidences that seem to guide you along your path. You might start noticing repeating numbers, running into people who help you on your journey, or experiencing events that feel too perfectly timed to be mere coincidence. These synchronicities are signs that you are aligned with the flow of the universe and are on the right path.

In 4D consciousness, you begin to recognize that life is always communicating with you through these subtle messages. The more open and aware you are, the more synchronicities you will experience. These moments serve as reminders that you are not alone on your journey and that the universe is always supporting your growth and evolution.

The Challenges of 4D Consciousness

While 4D consciousness is a time of awakening and expansion, it is also a phase filled with challenges. You may find yourself caught between the old 3D way of thinking and the new 5D perspective you are moving toward. This can create moments of confusion, doubt, and fear as your old beliefs clash with your new understanding.

During this transition, you may feel more sensitive to the energies around you, noticing the emotions of others or feeling overwhelmed by negativity. You might also experience the dark night of the soul—a period of deep introspection and emotional turmoil as you confront the aspects of yourself and your life that need healing.

These challenges are a natural part of the process, and they are necessary for your growth. They help you shed the layers of conditioning that have kept you from fully embodying your true essence.

TIP:
Start each day with 5 minutes of mindfulness meditation.

QUESTIONS FOR CONTEMPLATION

What beliefs or societal norms have you recently questioned, and how has this shift changed your perspective?

How do you experience synchronicities, and what messages do you believe they hold for your spiritual journey?

In what ways have you noticed heightened sensitivity to others' emotions or energies? How can you create healthy boundaries to protect your energy while remaining open to growth?

Reflect on a shadow aspect of yourself that has surfaced recently. How can you begin to embrace and integrate this part of yourself with compassion?

What does your intuition tell you about your current path, and how can you strengthen your connection to this inner guidance?

Notes

chapter 5

5D CONSCIOUSNESS - A NEW PARADIGM

"IN THE FIFTH DIMENSION, LOVE AND UNITY BECOME THE GUIDING PRINCIPLES, AND THE ILLUSION OF SEPARATION DISSOLVES INTO ONENESS."
– ZEN

The shift into 5D consciousness is often described as entering a new paradigm of being. In this state, life is experienced through the lens of unconditional love, unity, and interconnectedness. It represents a profound shift from the ego-driven, dualistic nature of 3D and the transitional healing phase of 4D. In 5D, individuals move beyond the need for external validation and control, embracing a heart-centered existence that is guided by compassion, intuition, and a deep sense of oneness with all that is.

At its core, 5D consciousness is characterized by living from the heart. Decisions are no longer based on fear, survival, or personal gain, but rather on love, empathy, and collective well-being. In this dimension, individuals feel a deep sense of peace and trust, understanding that life unfolds in divine timing and that each experience, whether joyful or challenging, serves a higher purpose. The attachment to rigid outcomes and expectations dissolves, replaced by a sense of flow and surrender. Life becomes less about achieving and more about aligning—with the higher self, with love, and with the natural rhythm of the universe.

In 5D consciousness, the illusion of separation fades, replaced by an awareness of unity. Individuals realize that they are not isolated beings, but part of a greater whole that includes other people, nature, and the cosmos. This sense of oneness fosters a genuine desire to contribute to the well-being of others, as acts of kindness and service are seen as extensions of self-love. Compassion flows naturally, not as an obligation but as a spontaneous expression of the heart's essence.

Relationships transform in this dimension, becoming more authentic, fulfilling, and based on mutual growth rather than need or dependency.

Manifestation in 5D is not about forcing outcomes but co-creating with the universe. As individuals align their thoughts, emotions, and actions with higher vibrations, they attract experiences that resonate with their true essence. It's a process that involves clear intentions, deep trust, and a willingness to release attachment to specific results. People in 5D understand that they are active participants in shaping reality and that their inner state directly influences the external world. This awareness brings a sense of empowerment, as individuals realize that they can create a life of love, abundance, and joy by aligning with their highest self.

Intuition plays a central role in 5D consciousness, serving as a reliable guide for decision-making and daily interactions.

Individuals in this dimension trust their inner knowing more than external advice, feeling a direct connection to their higher self and spiritual guidance. This intuitive awareness extends beyond the self, often manifesting as telepathic communication, premonitions, or a heightened ability to perceive energy.

As intuition becomes more refined, people feel more aligned with their soul's purpose, navigating life with a sense of clarity and grace.

While 5D consciousness is often associated with bliss, it does not mean the absence of challenges. Instead, challenges are viewed as opportunities for growth, reflection, and further alignment. Individuals no longer see obstacles as personal failures but as invitations to deepen their understanding and elevate their consciousness. This perspective fosters resilience, as setbacks are met with compassion and curiosity rather than resistance or self-blame.

Anchoring 5D consciousness requires daily practices that align the body, mind, and spirit. Meditation, heart-centered breathing, gratitude rituals, and acts of service are effective ways to maintain a high vibration. Spending time in nature, connecting with animals, or engaging in creative activities also supports the embodiment of 5D energy. The focus is always on living from the heart, nurturing inner peace, and contributing to the collective awakening of humanity

Living from the Heart

In 5D, you begin to operate not from the mind and ego, but from the heart. The heart is the center of love, compassion, and intuition. It is through the heart that you connect to your higher self and to others in a meaningful, authentic way. In 3D, decisions are often made from fear or logic, but in 5D, decisions are made from a place of love, based on what feels right in alignment with your soul.

When you live from the heart, you radiate love and compassion toward yourself and others. Judgment and criticism fall away as you recognize that everyone is on their own journey of growth and healing. You see beyond the surface, knowing that at the core, we are all connected by the same universal energy.

The heart-centered approach allows you to experience deep empathy and understanding, making you more open to helping others and building meaningful relationships. In this state, life becomes a flow of giving and receiving love, and this exchange brings peace and fulfillment to your everyday experience.

Unity Consciousness

A key aspect of 5D is unity consciousness. In 3D, there is a strong belief in separation—individuals see themselves as separate from others, from nature, and from the universe. But in 5D, this illusion of separation dissolves. You begin to see the interconnectedness of all things: the plants, the animals, the people, and the planet. Everything is part of the same web of life, and we all affect each other.

This realization transforms how you interact with the world. You start to see that the well-being of others is as important as your own, and you naturally begin to live in a way that honors the Earth, animals, and people around you. Compassion and kindness flow effortlessly because you know that by serving others, you are serving yourself.

Unity consciousness is about recognizing that the universe is not just something outside of you but is within you. You are a part of the universal energy that creates everything. This knowledge brings a deep sense of peace, knowing that you are never alone, never separate. Every thought, emotion, and action you take contributes to the collective consciousness, raising the frequency of the planet.

The Power of Intuition

In 5D consciousness, you begin to trust your intuition as a guiding force in your life. Unlike 3D, where decisions are made based on logic or external validation, in 5D you listen to your inner knowing. Your higher self communicates through your intuition, nudging you in the direction of your soul's purpose.
You may notice that in 5D, your intuition becomes clearer and stronger. You start to receive subtle messages from the universe—whether through dreams, synchronicities, or gut feelings. Trusting this guidance allows you to move through life with ease and flow, knowing that you are always supported and aligned with your highest good.
Intuition in 5D consciousness is more than just making decisions; it's about living in constant dialogue with the universe. The more you tune in and trust, the more you will experience a life of harmony and purpose. You learn to surrender control, knowing that your soul is leading the way.

Manifesting from 5D

One of the most profound shifts in 5D consciousness is the ability to manifest your reality from a place of alignment. In 3D, manifesting often involves hard work, effort, and a constant struggle to get what you want. In 5D, manifestation becomes an effortless process because you are in tune with the universe's flow. Your desires are no longer driven by ego but by your soul's true purpose.

In 5D, you manifest from a state of abundance and gratitude, knowing that the universe always provides what you need when you are aligned with love and purpose. You no longer feel the need to "force" things to happen. Instead, you set your intention and trust that the right opportunities, people, and resources will flow into your life at the perfect time.

Key to manifesting in 5D:

• Align your vibration with love: Manifest from a place of gratitude and trust, rather than fear or lack.
• Set clear intentions: Focus on what feels aligned with your soul, not just your ego's desires.
• Trust the process: Allow things to unfold without trying to control the outcome. Trust that what is meant for you will come in divine timing.

Expanding Awareness

In 5D consciousness, your awareness expands beyond the physical realm. You begin to perceive life from a multi-dimensional perspective, understanding that there is more to reality than meets the eye. You might experience moments of profound clarity where you can sense the energy of others, communicate with your higher self, or receive insights from the universe.

This expanded awareness allows you to tap into higher frequencies of love, joy, and peace. You start to notice the beauty in everyday moments, whether it's the sound of the wind, the warmth of the sun, or the connection with another human being. In 5D, every moment becomes an opportunity for spiritual growth and connection.

Through this heightened awareness, you begin to see that life is not happening to you but for you. Every experience, challenge, and person you encounter is part of your soul's journey, offering lessons that help you evolve. In this state, you no longer see problems as obstacles but as opportunities for growth and expansion.

How to Maintain 5D Consciousness

While 5D consciousness brings immense peace and clarity, it is not a static state. It requires conscious effort to stay aligned with these higher frequencies, especially in a world that is still largely rooted in 3D. Here are some key practices to help you maintain 5D consciousness:

1. Daily Meditation and Mindfulness: Quiet your mind and connect with your higher self through meditation. This helps you stay grounded and aligned with your soul.

2. Practice Gratitude: Regularly reflect on the blessings in your life. Gratitude raises your vibration and keeps you aligned with abundance.

3. Surround Yourself with High-Vibe People: Engage with people who support your growth and share your vision of unity and love. Community is essential in maintaining 5D awareness.

4. Follow Your Joy: In 5D, joy is a sign that you are aligned with your higher self. Follow the activities and passions that bring you joy, and let go of anything that feels heavy or misaligned.

5. Stay Open to Growth: Remember, the journey of consciousness is ongoing. Stay open to learning, evolving, and expanding into even higher dimensions of awareness.

Affirmations for Manifesting

"I am a powerful creator, and I attract abundance and opportunities effortlessly."

"The universe aligns with my intentions, and everything I desire flows to me with ease."

"I am grateful for the manifestations unfolding in my life, bringing me closer to my dreams."

QUESTIONS FOR CONTEMPLATION

How do you currently experience living from the heart, and how can you deepen this practice in your daily life?

Reflect on a recent experience where you felt a sense of oneness with another person, nature, or the universe. What did this experience teach you about unity?

How do you approach challenges in your life? Are you able to see them as opportunities for growth and alignment, or do you view them as setbacks?

What intentions do you hold for co-creating your reality, and how can you align more deeply with these intentions while remaining open to divine timing?

How can you serve others in a way that feels aligned with your heart, contributing to the collective well-being?

Notes

Part 2

INNER TRANSFORMATION AND HEALING

chapter 6

EVOLVING YOUR ESSENCE. EGO VS. SPIRITUAL SELF: RECOGNIZING THE INNER BATTLE

"TRUE EVOLUTION BEGINS WHEN WE ALIGN WITH OUR INNER ESSENCE, TRANSCENDING THE LIMITS OF WHO WE THOUGHT WE WERE."
– ZEN

Evolving your essence is a deeply personal and transformative process that involves reconnecting with your true self. It's about stripping away the layers of conditioning, societal expectations, and ego-based identities to uncover who you are at your core. As you evolve, you begin to align more closely with your soul's purpose, discovering what truly fulfills you on a spiritual, emotional, and physical level. This evolution is not about becoming something new, but rather about returning to the essence of who you have always been—your authentic, unconditioned self.

At the heart of essence evolution is the practice of self-discovery. It requires courage to look inward and face the parts of yourself that have been suppressed or ignored. This process is not always easy, as it often involves confronting fears, past traumas, and limiting beliefs that have shaped your reality. However, it is also liberating, offering the opportunity to reclaim your power and step into a more authentic version of yourself. Through practices like meditation, journaling, and deep reflection, you begin to peel back the layers of the false self and make space for your true essence to emerge.

Releasing limiting beliefs is a critical part of evolving your essence. These beliefs, often formed in childhood or early adulthood, create a sense of restriction and prevent you from living fully. For example, beliefs like "I am not good enough," "I have to please others to be loved," or "Success is only achieved through hard work and struggle" are common barriers to self-realization.

By identifying and reframing these beliefs, you open yourself to new possibilities and align with your higher truth. Reframing involves replacing negative self-talk with affirmations that empower and uplift you, creating a new narrative that supports your growth.

As you evolve, your relationship with purpose also transforms. No longer is purpose tied to external achievements or societal definitions of success. Instead, it becomes a matter of alignment—finding what brings you joy, fulfillment, and a sense of contribution. Your soul's purpose is often revealed through passions and interests that have been present throughout your life but may have been overshadowed by obligations or fears. It's about following what lights you up, trusting that your gifts are meant to be shared, and allowing your passions to guide your path. This alignment creates a life that feels meaningful, regardless of the external outcomes.

The journey of evolving your essence is also about cultivating self-love and compassion. It involves treating yourself with kindness, understanding, and acceptance, even when facing setbacks or imperfections. Self-love is not just about pampering or positive affirmations—it is about embracing all parts of yourself, including the flaws and shadows, with tenderness and grace. This compassionate approach fosters a sense of inner peace and stability, creating a foundation from which authentic growth can flourish.

Living authentically is a hallmark of essence evolution. It means being true to yourself in all areas of life, whether in relationships, career, or personal beliefs.

Authenticity requires vulnerability—the willingness to be seen for who you truly are, without masks or pretenses. It involves setting boundaries that protect your energy and honor your needs, even if it means disappointing others. By living authentically, you create a ripple effect that encourages others to do the same, contributing to a more honest and connected world. Spiritual practices play a significant role in evolving your essence. Meditation, breathwork, and other forms of inner work help maintain a connection to your higher self, offering insights and guidance along the way. Gratitude, too, is a powerful tool, as it shifts focus from lack to abundance, helping you appreciate the beauty of who you are and the journey you're on. As you engage in these practices consistently, you reinforce the alignment with your true essence, making it easier to navigate challenges and stay connected to your purpose.

The path of evolving your essence is not always linear. There will be moments of doubt, resistance, and confusion. Yet, these moments are also opportunities for deeper healing and integration. Each challenge, whether internal or external, serves as a mirror, reflecting the areas where further growth is needed. The key is to approach these experiences with curiosity rather than judgment, seeing them as invitations to expand rather than obstacles to overcome.

Ego vs. Spiritual Self

The concept of the ego vs. the spiritual self lies at the heart of spiritual awakening and personal growth. The ego, often misunderstood, is not inherently negative; rather, it is a construct of the mind designed to protect, define, and separate us. It is shaped by our experiences, identities, and societal influences, creating a sense of "self" that is rooted in fear, comparison, and attachment to the external world. The ego thrives on control, validation, and the illusion of individuality, often keeping us stuck in patterns of insecurity, judgment, and limitation.

In contrast, the spiritual self represents the eternal, unchanging essence within each of us. It is the part of us that is connected to universal consciousness, love, and unity. The spiritual self is expansive and unbound by the constructs of time, space, or identity. It operates from a place of intuition, compassion, and alignment with higher truths. Unlike the ego, the spiritual self does not seek validation from the outside world because it inherently knows its worth and connection to something greater.

Understanding the dynamic between the ego and the spiritual self is essential for awakening. The goal is not to destroy the ego but to recognize its role and learn to transcend its control. Through mindfulness, self-awareness, and spiritual practices, we can identify when the ego is driving our thoughts and actions, allowing the spiritual self to lead instead.

This shift requires a conscious effort to release attachments, let go of fear-based thinking, and trust in the flow of life. It's about embracing vulnerability, authenticity, and the realization that we are not separate beings but interconnected expressions of a greater whole.

In essence, the journey from ego to spiritual self is one of remembering who we truly are beyond the labels and illusions of the material world. It is a path of integration, where the ego becomes a servant of the soul rather than its master, paving the way for profound inner peace and alignment with our highest purpose.

Common Traits of the Ego
- **Fear and Insecurity:** The ego often operates from a place of fear, seeking control or external validation to feel secure.
- **Comparison and Competition:** It thrives on measuring itself against others, leading to judgment or jealousy.
- **Attachment to Roles and Labels:** The ego identifies with external markers like job titles, possessions, or social status.
- **Resistance to Change:** It clings to comfort zones and fears the unknown.
- **Illusion of Separation:** The ego sees itself as distinct and isolated from others and the universe.
-

2. Common Traits of the Spiritual Self
- **Inner Peace and Trust:** The spiritual self embodies calmness and trust in the unfolding of life.
- **Compassion and Unity:** It recognizes the interconnectedness of all beings and acts with empathy.

- Authenticity and Purpose: The spiritual self aligns actions with inner truth rather than external pressures.
- Openness and Growth: It welcomes change as an opportunity for evolution.
- Timeless Awareness: The spiritual self transcends the need for external validation, recognizing its inherent worth.

3. The Role of the Ego in Personal Growth
Instead of demonizing the ego, highlight its utility:
- The ego serves as a tool for navigating the physical world, providing a sense of individuality needed for certain life experiences.
- Challenges created by the ego (like fear or conflict) are opportunities for spiritual growth and self-discovery.
- The goal is to balance the ego's practical role with the guidance of the spiritual self, using the ego as a servant rather than a master.

4. Practical Ways to Transcend the Ego
Offer actionable steps readers can take:
- Mindfulness Practices: Cultivate present-moment awareness to observe ego-driven thoughts without attachment.
- Gratitude Journaling: Shift focus from lack (ego's perspective) to abundance (spiritual perspective).
- Meditation: Connect with the spiritual self by quieting the mind and accessing deeper awareness.

- Shadow Work: Address unconscious fears, insecurities, and patterns tied to the ego.
- Acts of Service: Engage in selfless actions to dissolve the illusion of separation.

5. Examples of Ego vs. Spiritual Self in Action
   - Illustrate the concepts with real-life scenarios:
   - Ego Response: Feeling angry and defensive when criticized.
   - Spiritual Self Response: Viewing criticism as an opportunity for reflection and growth.
   - Ego Perspective: "I need to achieve this to be worthy."
   - Spiritual Self Perspective: "I am worthy as I am, and achievement is an expression of my passion."
   - Ego Reaction: Comparing your progress to others and feeling inadequate.
   - Spiritual Self Reaction: Celebrating others' successes and trusting your unique path.

6. The Process of Integration
   - Explain how the ego and spiritual self can coexist:
   - Integration is about harmonizing the two, allowing the spiritual self to lead while the ego plays a supportive role.
   - Instead of rejecting the ego, acknowledge its presence with compassion, understanding it as a part of the human experience.
   - Example: Using the ego's drive for achievement to pursue a passion aligned with the spiritual self's purpose.

7. Key Practices for Awakening the Spiritual Self
- Daily Affirmations: Reinforce spiritual truths (e.g., "I am connected to the infinite wisdom within me.").
- Detachment from Outcomes: Practice surrender by focusing on effort rather than clinging to results.
- Nature Immersion: Spend time in nature to dissolve the ego's sense of separation and reconnect with universal energy.
- Self-Inquiry: Ask reflective questions like, "Who am I beyond my thoughts, roles, and emotions?".
- Mindfulness Activities: we will cover this more in depth in another chapter

8. Signs You Are Shifting from Ego to Spiritual Self
- Help readers recognize progress:
- Greater self-awareness and reduced reactivity.
- A shift from competition to collaboration.
- Increased empathy and less judgment of self and others.
- More focus on internal fulfillment than external validation.
- A sense of ease, flow, and alignment with life's purpose.

You Are Not Your Mind
- Understanding the Mind: The mind is a powerful tool, but it is not the essence of who we are. It functions as a program, processing information and creating thoughts based on past experiences and conditioning. However, our true identity lies beyond these mental constructs.

- Reprogramming the Mind: Just as a computer program can be updated, we can reprogram our minds to align with our spiritual self. This involves changing thought patterns and beliefs that no longer serve us. Techniques such as affirmations, visualization, and mindfulness can help in this reprogramming process.
- Steps to Disidentify from the Mind
    - Observe and Detach: Begin by observing your thoughts without judgment. Recognize that you are the observer, not the thoughts themselves.
    - Cultivate Awareness: Practice mindfulness to stay present and aware of your mental activity. This helps in identifying when the ego is in control.
    - Develop a Witness Consciousness: Strengthen your ability to witness your thoughts and emotions without becoming entangled in them. This creates space for the spiritual self to emerge.

Understanding the distinction between the ego self and the spiritual self is a vital step in the journey of awakening. By recognizing the ego's limitations and embracing the qualities of the spiritual self, we can live more authentic, fulfilling lives. Remember, you are not your mind; you are the consciousness that observes and transcends it. Embrace your journey with love, compassion, and authenticity, knowing that every step you take brings you closer to your true self.

QUESTIONS FOR CONTEMPLATION

What beliefs about yourself have you recently questioned, and how has this shift impacted your sense of self?

How do you define your soul's purpose, and what steps can you take to align more fully with it in your daily life?

In what areas of your life are you still seeking external validation? How can you begin to validate yourself from within?

Reflect on a recent moment of authenticity. How did it feel to express your true self, and what was the response from others?

How can you cultivate greater self-love and compassion during this phase of your journey?

Notes

chapter 7

LETTING GO OF 3D ATTACHMENTS

"FREEDOM IS FOUND NOT IN HOLDING ON, BUT IN RELEASING THE WEIGHT OF WHAT NO LONGER SERVES YOUR HIGHER SELF."
– ZEN

Letting go of 3D attachments is a pivotal step in the journey toward higher consciousness. The attachments that define 3D consciousness are rooted in the material world, ego-based desires, and a need for control. These attachments are not inherently wrong, but they can be limiting when they prevent deeper spiritual growth and alignment with one's true essence. Releasing them allows individuals to shift from a mindset of scarcity and fear to one of abundance and love, paving the way for more profound personal transformation.

At its core, 3D attachment is tied to a sense of identity that is based on external achievements, possessions, and validation from others. It involves clinging to labels—such as success, wealth, beauty, or status—that are defined by societal norms. This attachment creates a cycle of striving, where fulfillment is sought outside of oneself, often leading to stress, anxiety, and a constant sense of inadequacy. As individuals begin to awaken to higher dimensions of consciousness, they recognize that these attachments no longer serve them. They start to understand that true fulfillment comes from within, from alignment with the soul, rather than from external sources.

Letting go of 3D attachments involves a process of unlearning. It requires examining beliefs, patterns, and behaviors that have been shaped by the desire to fit in, succeed, or be accepted by others. This process can be challenging, as it often means confronting fears of rejection, failure, or loss. It is natural to feel resistance during this stage, as the ego perceives these changes as threats to its sense of identity and security.

However, by facing these fears with compassion and a willingness to evolve, individuals can begin to release the need for approval, validation, and control.

One of the most significant attachments in 3D is to material wealth. In a society that equates success with financial status, the pursuit of money can become an end in itself rather than a means to create freedom, joy, or contribution. Releasing the attachment to money does not mean abandoning financial goals; rather, it means shifting the focus from accumulation to alignment. Money becomes a tool for living in alignment with one's purpose, rather than a measure of self-worth. By cultivating a mindset of abundance, individuals learn to trust that their needs will be met as they align with their higher self.

Another common attachment in 3D consciousness is to roles and identities. People often define themselves by their careers, relationships, or societal roles, such as being a parent, partner, or professional. While these roles are important, they are not the entirety of who you are. Letting go of rigid identification with roles allows for greater flexibility and freedom. It opens up space for exploring other aspects of the self and creates room for personal growth. This release is not about abandoning responsibilities but about recognizing that your essence transcends any single role or label.

Control is another key attachment in 3D consciousness. The desire to control outcomes, situations, or even other people often stems from fear and a lack of trust in the natural flow of life.

Letting go of control involves embracing uncertainty and surrendering to the idea that the universe has a divine plan.

This does not mean becoming passive or inactive; rather, it means aligning with the flow of life and trusting that things will unfold as they are meant to. Surrendering control allows for greater peace, as it reduces anxiety and the need to micromanage every aspect of life.

Letting go of attachments also extends to relationships. In 3D consciousness, relationships are often based on dependency, need, or fear of being alone. As individuals evolve, they realize that true connection is not about possession or control but about mutual growth, support, and freedom. Releasing attachment in relationships means loving others unconditionally, without trying to change them or mold them to fit personal desires. It involves allowing others to be their true selves, even if it means parting ways when growth takes different directions.

The process of letting go is not a one-time event but a continuous practice. It requires daily awareness, reflection, and a commitment to inner freedom. It is helpful to engage in practices like meditation, journaling, and breathwork to support this release. These practices help quiet the mind, create inner stillness, and allow for deeper insights into what attachments are holding you back. As you let go of what no longer serves you, you make room for new possibilities, growth, and alignment with your higher self.

QUESTIONS FOR CONTEMPLATION

What material possessions, roles, or achievements do you currently feel attached to, and how do they define your sense of self?

In what ways has the need for control impacted your relationships, decisions, or well-being? How can you practice surrender and trust in daily life?

Reflect on a recent situation where you sought external validation. What underlying belief fueled this need, and how can you begin to validate yourself from within?

How do you define abundance? What steps can you take to cultivate an abundance mindset that is not tied solely to financial gain?

How can you create healthier, more unconditional relationships by releasing expectations and embracing freedom for yourself and others?

Notes

chapter 8

Healing and Integration

"Healing is not about fixing; it is about remembering and reclaiming all parts of yourself as whole."
– Zen

Healing and integration are central to the journey of awakening consciousness. As individuals transition from the ego-driven state of 3D to the heart-centered awareness of 5D, they encounter layers of wounds, traumas, and limiting beliefs that have shaped their sense of self and reality. The process of healing involves bringing these hidden aspects to light, understanding their origins, and integrating them with compassion. It is through this deep inner work that individuals can achieve wholeness and create a foundation for living in alignment with their higher selves.

At the core of healing is the concept of integration—embracing all parts of oneself, including those that have been rejected, suppressed, or deemed unworthy. Often, these shadow aspects were formed in response to painful experiences, unmet needs, or societal conditioning. The ego, seeking to protect the self, pushes these aspects into the subconscious, where they continue to influence behavior, thoughts, and emotions. As individuals awaken, these shadows rise to the surface, demanding attention and healing.

The process of shadow integration requires honesty, vulnerability, and a willingness to confront uncomfortable truths. It involves recognizing the parts of oneself that have been hidden in the shadows, whether they manifest as anger, fear, jealousy, or shame. By bringing these aspects into conscious awareness, individuals can begin to understand the roots of their behavior and beliefs.

For example, someone may realize that their tendency to avoid conflict stems from a fear of rejection developed during childhood. As this realization takes hold, it creates an opportunity to heal the underlying wound and change the behavior.

Healing is not limited to shadow work; it also involves addressing unresolved traumas that are stored in the body. Trauma, whether physical or emotional, leaves imprints on the nervous system, creating patterns of reactivity, anxiety, or disconnection. Practices like somatic experiencing, breathwork, or energy healing can be effective tools for releasing trauma from the body, allowing for a more integrated and harmonious state of being. By working through these layers of pain and tension, individuals can free themselves from past influences and open up to a more authentic way of living.

Another vital aspect of healing is inner child work. The inner child represents the parts of the self that carry childhood wounds, unmet needs, and unfulfilled desires. Connecting with the inner child is a powerful way to heal old wounds and nurture a sense of safety, love, and belonging. This process often involves visualizations, dialogues, and affirmations that reassure the inner child of their worth and safety. As the inner child heals, individuals experience greater emotional stability, self-compassion, and a sense of wholeness.

The integration process is not only about healing wounds but also about uniting the masculine and feminine energies within.

These energies, often referred to as the sacred masculine and sacred feminine, exist in every individual, regardless of gender. The sacred masculine represents qualities like strength, action, and structure, while the sacred feminine embodies intuition, nurturing, and receptivity. Integration involves balancing these energies, allowing for a more complete expression of the self. For example, someone may realize that they have been overly focused on achieving goals (masculine energy) while neglecting rest and self-care (feminine energy). By integrating both energies, individuals can create a more harmonious inner state and a balanced approach to life.

Healing and integration are ongoing processes that require patience, persistence, and self-compassion. It is not a linear path; rather, it is a spiral of growth where old wounds may resurface at deeper levels, offering new layers of healing. The key is to approach each challenge with curiosity rather than judgment, understanding that healing is a journey, not a destination. As individuals heal and integrate, they become more aligned with their true essence, creating a solid foundation for spiritual growth and higher states of consciousness.

TIP: Spend time in nature to reconnect with your inner wisdom.

QUESTIONS FOR CONTEMPLATION

What aspects of yourself have you struggled to accept, and how can you begin to embrace them with compassion?

Reflect on a past trauma that continues to influence your behavior or emotions. What steps can you take to heal this trauma at a deeper level?

How can you connect with your inner child, and what messages does your inner child need to hear to feel safe and loved?

In what ways have you noticed an imbalance between your masculine and feminine energies?

How can you create a more harmonious balance between action and intuition in your life?

What practices or rituals can you incorporate into your daily routine to support ongoing healing and integration?

Notes

chapter 9

SHADOW INTEGRATION: EMBRACING THE HIDDEN PARTS OF YOU

"EMBRACING YOUR SHADOW IS NOT ABOUT FIGHTING DARKNESS, BUT ABOUT RECLAIMING THE LIGHT HIDDEN WITHIN IT."
– ZEN

Shadow integration is a transformative aspect of the journey toward awakening consciousness. The "shadow" represents the parts of the self that have been repressed, denied, or hidden due to fear, shame, or social conditioning. These aspects often reside in the subconscious and can manifest as fears, unresolved traumas, limiting beliefs, or undesirable traits. While the shadow is often perceived negatively, it is not inherently "bad." It holds valuable insights, unclaimed power, and unhealed wounds that, when integrated, lead to greater wholeness, authenticity, and self-awareness.

The first step in shadow integration is acknowledging the shadow's presence. This requires self-awareness and honesty, as it involves looking at aspects of yourself that may be uncomfortable or difficult to accept. The shadow often reveals itself through triggers—situations or people that provoke strong emotional reactions, such as anger, jealousy, or fear. For example, if someone's confidence triggers feelings of inadequacy within you, it may be a sign that your own sense of self-worth needs attention. Recognizing these triggers as mirrors rather than threats is the foundation of shadow work.

Self-reflection is a key part of integrating the shadow. It involves examining your thoughts, behaviors, and emotional patterns to identify underlying fears, beliefs, or traumas that may be rooted in the shadow. Journaling is a helpful tool for this process, as it allows for honest exploration of thoughts and feelings without judgment. By writing about your experiences, triggers, or recurring patterns, you can bring the unconscious to light and begin to understand how the shadow influences your decisions and relationships.

Another important aspect of shadow integration is accepting the shadow without judgment. The goal is not to eliminate or suppress the shadow but to embrace it as part of your wholeness. This acceptance requires compassion and a willingness to understand the shadow's origins—often linked to childhood experiences, societal conditioning, or trauma. For example, someone who was taught that anger is unacceptable may suppress their anger, leading to passive-aggressive behavior or internalized resentment. By acknowledging and allowing the anger to surface in a safe and controlled way, they can integrate this emotion and express it healthily.

Inner child work is closely connected to shadow integration, as many shadow aspects originate in childhood. The inner child holds both the innocence and the wounds of the past, influencing adult behavior and beliefs. Reconnecting with the inner child through visualization, dialogue, or creative activities helps address unresolved wounds and reclaim the parts of the self that were abandoned or rejected. This process often involves offering the inner child love, reassurance, and validation, which promotes healing and integration.

Forgiveness is also a powerful component of shadow work. It involves forgiving not only others who may have contributed to the formation of the shadow but also yourself for suppressing or denying these parts.

Forgiveness is not about condoning harmful behavior but about releasing the hold of resentment, guilt, or shame. This release creates space for compassion, both for yourself and others, and allows for a more complete integration of all aspects of the self.

Meditation and visualization are effective practices for integrating the shadow. During meditation, you can invite the shadow to reveal itself in a non-threatening way, asking questions like, "What do you want me to know?" or "How can I heal this aspect of myself?" Visualization can be used to imagine the shadow as a figure or symbol, engaging in a dialogue to understand its purpose and needs. This compassionate approach helps dissolve the fear and resistance that often accompany shadow work, making it easier to embrace the shadow as a valuable part of your journey.

Another helpful tool is shadow journaling, a practice where you write from the perspective of the shadow. This exercise involves letting the shadow "speak" on the page, expressing its thoughts, fears, and desires without censorship. By giving the shadow a voice, you can gain insights into its motivations and unmet needs, which can then be addressed through conscious actions and choices. For example, if the shadow expresses a fear of rejection, you might work on building self-acceptance or strengthening boundaries in relationships.

Projection is a common way that the shadow manifests in daily life. Projection occurs when you attribute your own suppressed feelings or traits to others, often criticizing or resenting them for these qualities. For example, someone who denies their own need for recognition might criticize others for seeking attention. Recognizing and reclaiming these projections is a key part of shadow integration, as it involves taking responsibility for your own emotions and actions. This reclamation creates greater self-awareness, reducing judgment and increasing empathy for others.

As you work on integrating the shadow, it's essential to practice self-care and grounding. Shadow work can be emotionally intense, bringing up old wounds or uncomfortable feelings. Engaging in self-care practices like mindfulness, grounding exercises, or spending time in nature helps maintain emotional stability and balance. It also ensures that you remain centered as you explore deeper layers of the subconscious.

The integration of the shadow ultimately leads to greater authenticity and wholeness. By embracing all aspects of the self, including those that were once hidden or rejected, you can live more authentically, relate to others more compassionately, and align more deeply with your true essence. Shadow work is not a one-time process but an ongoing journey that supports personal growth and spiritual evolution.

QUESTIONS FOR CONTEMPLATION

What triggers have you experienced recently, and how do they reveal hidden aspects of your shadow?

How can you approach the shadow with compassion rather than judgment, allowing it to express itself safely and honestly?

What childhood wounds or experiences might be linked to your current shadow aspects, and how can you begin to heal them through inner child work?

How do you experience projection in your relationships? Are there qualities you criticize in others that may reflect unclaimed parts of yourself?

What self-care practices can support you during the process of shadow integration, helping you stay grounded and centered?

NOTES

chapter 10

Inner Child Healing: Reconnecting with Your Authentic Self

"Healing the inner child is not about changing the past but about giving yourself the love and safety you deserved all along."
— Zen

Inner child healing is a vital part of the journey to higher consciousness. It involves reconnecting with and nurturing the younger, wounded parts of yourself that have often been ignored, repressed, or forgotten. The inner child represents not only the memories and emotions of your early years but also your core sense of innocence, wonder, and creativity. It is the part of you that still carries the unhealed wounds from childhood—unmet needs, unresolved traumas, and limiting beliefs that were formed at a young age. By healing the inner child, you can release these patterns and create a more loving, compassionate, and authentic relationship with yourself.

The first step in inner child healing is acknowledging that this part of you exists and holds significant influence over your thoughts, feelings, and behaviors. Often, the inner child's wounds manifest as fears of abandonment, rejection, or unworthiness. These fears can shape adult relationships, self-perception, and even career choices, leading to patterns of people-pleasing, self-sabotage, or avoidance of intimacy. By becoming aware of the inner child's presence and recognizing its impact, you open the door to a deeper level of healing and self-awareness. Reconnecting with the inner child requires creating a safe, non-judgmental space for it to express itself. This can be done through practices like visualization, journaling, or dialogue. Visualization involves closing your eyes, relaxing your body, and imagining your younger self standing before you. In this space, you can have a conversation with your inner child, asking questions like, "What do you need from me?" or "How can I help you feel safe and loved?". This process helps build trust between your adult self and the inner child, allowing for a more authentic connection. Journaling is another powerful tool for inner child healing. Writing letters to your younger self, expressing compassion, understanding, and love, can help release pent-up emotions and provide validation that was missing in childhood. You can also use journaling to explore specific memories, acknowledging the feelings and experiences that were suppressed at the time. This process allows for the release of old pain and helps integrate the inner child's perspective with your current awareness.

Dialogue, whether spoken aloud or written, is a direct way to communicate with the inner child. It involves asking your inner child how they are feeling, what they need, and what fears or beliefs they are holding onto. By responding with love, reassurance, and support, you create a healing dynamic that fosters safety and trust. This dialogue can be particularly effective in moments of stress, anxiety, or self-doubt, as it helps address the root causes of these feelings rather than just the symptoms.

Healing the inner child is not just about addressing wounds; it is also about reclaiming the joy, creativity, and sense of wonder that were present in childhood. As you heal, you begin to remember the things that once brought you happiness—play, imagination, and simple pleasures that have been overshadowed by adult responsibilities.

By embracing your inner child's capacity for joy, you can bring more playfulness and spontaneity into your life, enhancing your overall sense of well-being and alignment with your true essence.

Inner child healing is a gradual process that requires patience, consistency, and self-compassion. It is not about erasing the past but about integrating it with love and understanding. As you heal the inner child, you begin to experience greater emotional resilience, self-worth, and inner peace. You also develop a stronger foundation for deeper relationships, as your ability to give and receive love becomes more authentic and unconditional. This healing creates a ripple effect, positively influencing every aspect of your life and supporting your evolution toward higher states of consciousness.

Affirmations for healing your inner child

"I am safe, loved, and nurtured as I embrace my inner child with compassion and understanding."

"I release the past and honor the innocence, joy, and creativity within me."

"I give myself permission to heal, grow, and rewrite my story with love and acceptance."

QUESTIONS FOR CONTEMPLATION

Reflect on a childhood memory that still holds emotional charge for you. What does your inner child need to hear or receive to heal from this experience?

In what ways have your childhood wounds shaped your beliefs, behaviors, or relationships as an adult?

How can you create a safe, loving space for your inner child to express itself, and what specific actions can you take to nurture this part of you?

What activities or experiences brought you joy as a child, and how can you reintroduce these elements into your adult life?

How can you approach your inner child with compassion and understanding, even during moments of fear, anger, or sadness?

Notes

chapter 11

INTEGRATION OF PAST LIVES AND KARMA

"THE WISDOM OF PAST LIVES AND THE LESSONS OF KARMA WEAVE TOGETHER TO GUIDE THE SOUL'S JOURNEY TOWARD WHOLENESS."
– ZEN

The integration of past lives and karma is a profound aspect of spiritual awakening, offering insights into the patterns, lessons, and soul contracts that shape your current reality. From the perspective of consciousness, life is not limited to a single incarnation but unfolds across many lifetimes, each contributing to the evolution of the soul. Understanding past lives and karma allows for a deeper exploration of the self, uncovering unresolved energies, lessons, and talents that influence the present moment.

The concept of past lives is rooted in the belief that the soul is eternal, experiencing multiple incarnations to grow, learn, and evolve. Each lifetime is an opportunity for the soul to explore different experiences, relationships, and challenges. These lifetimes are interconnected, with unresolved issues, emotional wounds, or unlearned lessons carried over as karmic imprints. For example, patterns of fear, attachment, or recurring conflicts in relationships may be rooted in past-life experiences that remain unhealed or incomplete.

Karma, often misunderstood as punishment or reward, is more accurately described as the law of cause and effect. It reflects the energy created by thoughts, actions, and intentions across lifetimes, influencing current experiences and opportunities. Karma is not meant to be seen as a burden but as a mechanism for growth and learning. It provides opportunities to balance past actions, heal unresolved wounds, and cultivate higher states of consciousness. By becoming aware of karmic patterns, you can make conscious choices to transform them, creating a more aligned and fulfilling reality. Exploring past lives can offer valuable insights into your current life's themes, challenges, and gifts. Past-life regression, a therapeutic technique that uses hypnosis or deep meditation, allows individuals to access memories from previous incarnations. These memories often reveal unresolved issues or relationships that are playing out in the current life. For example, someone struggling with unexplained fears may discover a past-life trauma that created this energetic imprint. By acknowledging and healing these memories, individuals can release their hold, freeing themselves from limiting patterns.

Another way to access past-life information is through intuitive insights, dreams, or spontaneous memories that arise during meditation or moments of stillness. These glimpses of past lives can provide context for recurring themes, emotional triggers, or talents that seem innate. For example, an individual with a natural ability for music or art may be tapping into skills honed in previous lifetimes. Similarly, strong affinities or aversions to specific cultures, places, or people may indicate past-life connections that influence the present.

Healing karmic patterns involves a process of awareness, acceptance, and transformation. It begins with recognizing the patterns that repeat in your life—such as certain relationship dynamics, financial struggles, or self-sabotaging behaviors. These patterns often carry karmic energy that needs to be addressed and resolved. For example, someone who consistently experiences betrayal in relationships may be dealing with karmic lessons around trust and forgiveness. By bringing conscious awareness to these patterns, individuals can make different choices, align with higher intentions, and break free from karmic cycles. Forgiveness is a powerful tool for healing karma. It involves releasing resentment, guilt, or blame—whether directed toward others or oneself—that may be tied to past actions, both in this life and previous ones. Forgiveness is not about condoning harmful behavior but about freeing yourself from the energetic attachments that perpetuate suffering. It creates space for compassion, understanding, and the resolution of karmic debts, allowing for greater harmony and peace. Soul contracts are agreements made between souls before incarnating, often to facilitate specific lessons, growth, or experiences. These contracts can manifest as significant relationships, challenging situations, or even seemingly random encounters. Understanding the purpose of soul contracts helps individuals navigate life's challenges with greater acceptance and wisdom, recognizing that even difficult experiences serve a higher purpose. For example, a soul contract with a partner may involve learning lessons of love, patience, or boundaries, while a challenging work situation may be designed to teach perseverance or humility. Meditation, visualization, and journaling are effective practices for exploring past lives and karmic patterns. During meditation, you can set the intention to receive insights about a specific issue or pattern in your life, asking for guidance from your higher self or spiritual guides. Visualizations, such as imagining a doorway that leads to a past-life memory, can provide a deeper connection to your soul's history and the origins of karmic imprints. Journaling about recurring dreams, intuitive insights, or patterns in relationships can also help identify karmic themes that need healing. Integration of past lives and karma is not about dwelling in the past but about bringing awareness to how these influences shape your current reality. By understanding the lessons and unresolved energies from previous lifetimes, you can make more conscious choices, align with your soul's purpose, and create a reality that reflects your highest potential. This process fosters greater self-awareness, compassion, and spiritual growth, helping you transcend old patterns and evolve toward higher states of consciousness.

TIP: Journal daily to reflect on your thoughts and emotions.

QUESTIONS FOR CONTEMPLATION

What recurring patterns or themes have you noticed in your life, and how might they be connected to past-life experiences or karmic lessons?

How can you use forgiveness, both for yourself and others, as a tool for healing karmic imprints and creating a more harmonious reality?

Have you experienced dreams, memories, or intuitive insights that suggest a connection to past lives? What messages or lessons do they offer for your current path?

How can you honor the purpose of your soul contracts, even when they involve challenges or difficult relationships?

What practices, such as meditation or visualization, can support your exploration and healing of past lives and karma?

Notes

Part 3

PRACTICES FOR EVOLVING CONSCIOUSNESS

Chapter 12

RAISING YOUR VIBRATION: BECOMING A MAGNETIC FORCE FOR GOOD

"YOUR VIBRATION IS THE LANGUAGE OF YOUR SOUL; RAISE IT, AND THE UNIVERSE WILL LISTEN." – ZEN

Raising your vibration is about aligning your energy with higher frequencies of love, joy, and peace. Everything in the universe, including thoughts, emotions, and physical matter, vibrates at a particular frequency. When you consciously elevate your vibration, you become a powerful force for positive change—not just in your life, but in the world around you. A high vibration attracts similar energies, creating opportunities, relationships, and experiences that resonate with your highest good.

To begin raising your vibration, it's essential to cultivate awareness of your thoughts and emotions. Negative emotions like fear, anger, and guilt lower your vibration, while gratitude, compassion, and forgiveness elevate it. This doesn't mean avoiding difficult emotions; instead, acknowledge and process them with mindfulness, allowing them to move through you without lingering. Journaling, meditation, or simply sitting with your feelings can help you release low-vibrational energy and create space for healing.

Another key to elevating your vibration is the energy you consume—physically, mentally, and spiritually. Nourish your body with whole, natural foods that provide high-vibrational energy. Surround yourself with uplifting environments, supportive relationships, and content that inspires growth. Consider what you're reading, watching, or listening to, and choose inputs that resonate with positivity and wisdom.

Daily practices like meditation, breathwork, and gratitude journaling are transformative tools for raising your vibration. Meditation quiets the mind, allowing you to connect with your inner essence and align with universal energy. Gratitude journaling shifts your focus from lack to abundance, creating a magnetic field of positivity. Breathwork infuses your body with life force energy, clearing stagnant energy and raising your frequency. These practices help you stay present and connected to higher vibrational states.

Connection to nature is another powerful way to raise your vibration. The natural world vibrates at a pure, harmonious frequency, and spending time outdoors can help you recalibrate your energy. Walk barefoot on the earth, listen to the sound of waves, or simply sit beneath a tree to absorb nature's calming and rejuvenating energy. This connection reminds you of your place within the greater whole and helps you align with the natural flow of life.

As you raise your vibration, you'll notice subtle yet profound changes. Life begins to feel lighter, synchronicities occur more frequently, and you attract people and opportunities aligned with your purpose. You also become a beacon of light for others, radiating positivity that uplifts those around you. This ripple effect is the essence of being a magnetic force for good. By elevating your own energy, you inspire and empower others to do the same, contributing to the collective shift toward higher consciousness.

Ultimately, raising your vibration is a journey of self-awareness, intentionality, and alignment. It's about becoming the highest version of yourself, living authentically, and creating a life filled with meaning, love, and joy. By embracing this practice, you not only transform your own life but also become a powerful catalyst for positive change in the world.

Affirmations for Raising Your Vibration

"I radiate love, joy, and positivity in every aspect of my life."

"I align with the highest frequencies of peace, gratitude, and abundance."

"My energy is a magnet for harmony, growth, and limitless possibilities."

"I release all that no longer serves me and make space for higher vibrations to flow."

"With each breath, I elevate my vibration and connect with my true essence."

QUESTIONS FOR CONTEMPLATION

What thoughts, emotions, or habits are currently lowering my vibration, and how can I release them?

What practices or experiences consistently help me feel aligned, joyful, and at peace?

How can I consciously choose gratitude and love in moments of challenge or negativity?

What small, intentional steps can I take today to raise my vibration and positively impact those around me?

Notes

Chapter 13

Understanding Mindfulness: The Foundation of Awareness

"IN THE SYMPHONY OF EXISTENCE, HEALING BEGINS WHEN YOU ALIGN WITH THE FREQUENCY OF YOUR TRUE SELF." – ZEN

Understanding Mindfulness

Definition and History

Mindfulness is the practice of paying attention to the present moment with intention, while avoiding judgment. It is rooted in ancient contemplative traditions, particularly within Buddhism, where it has been a cornerstone of spiritual practice for over 2,500 years. In modern times, mindfulness has transcended its religious origins and has been widely adopted in secular contexts, thanks in part to the efforts of pioneers like Jon Kabat-Zinn, who developed the Mindfulness-Based Stress Reduction (MBSR) program in the late 1970s. This program has been instrumental in bringing mindfulness into mainstream medical and psychological practices.

Scientific Benefits of Mindfulness

The scientific community has conducted extensive research on mindfulness, uncovering a wide range of benefits. Studies have shown that mindfulness can significantly reduce stress, anxiety, and depression. It has been found to enhance emotional regulation, improve attention and focus, and boost overall well-being. Mindfulness practice is also associated with physical health benefits, such as reduced blood pressure, improved immune function, and better sleep. These findings highlight the profound impact mindfulness can have on both mental and physical health.

Mindfulness Practices

Meditation Techniques

- Breathing Meditation: Breathing meditation is one of the simplest and most accessible forms of mindfulness practice. It involves focusing on the breath as it flows in and out of the body. By paying close attention to each inhale and exhale, we can anchor ourselves in the present moment. When the mind wanders, as it inevitably will, we gently bring our focus back to the breath without judgment.
- Practice: Find a quiet place to sit comfortably. Close your eyes and take a few deep breaths. Then, allow your breathing to return to its natural rhythm. Focus on the sensation of the breath entering and leaving your nostrils or the rise and fall of your chest and abdomen. Continue this practice for 5-10 minutes, gradually extending the duration as you become more comfortable.
- Body Scan: The body scan is a mindfulness meditation that involves systematically focusing on different parts of the body, noticing any sensations without trying to change them. This practice helps cultivate a deeper awareness of physical presence and can be particularly effective in reducing tension and promoting relaxation.
- Practice: Lie down or sit comfortably with your eyes closed. Begin by bringing your attention to your toes, noticing any sensations there. Gradually move your focus up through your feet, legs, torso, arms, and head, spending a few moments on each area. If you

- notice any tension, acknowledge it without judgment and move on. The body scan can take 20-45 minutes, depending on how detailed you want to be.

Daily Mindfulness Routines
1. Mindful EatingMindful eating involves paying full attention to the experience of eating and drinking, both inside and outside the body. It encourages us to slow down and savor each bite, noticing the flavors, textures, and aromas of our food.
2. Practice: Start by taking a moment to appreciate the appearance and smell of your food. As you eat, chew slowly and notice the taste and texture. Pay attention to the sensations in your mouth and throat. Try to eat without distractions, such as watching TV or checking your phone.
3. Mindful WalkingMindful walking is a practice where we bring our full awareness to the act of walking, noticing each step and the sensations in our body. It can be a powerful way to integrate mindfulness into daily life.
4. Practice: Choose a place where you can walk undisturbed. Walk slowly and deliberately, paying attention to the movement of your feet and legs. Notice the feeling of the ground beneath you and the rhythm of your steps. If your mind wanders, gently bring your focus back to the act of walking.

Mindfulness in Everyday Life
- Incorporating Mindfulness into Work, Relationships, and Self-Care
- Mindfulness is not limited to formal meditation practices; it can be woven into the fabric of our daily lives. By bringing mindful awareness to our work, relationships, and self-care routines, we can enhance our overall quality of life.
- At Work: Mindfulness can improve productivity and reduce stress at work. By focusing on one task at a time and taking regular mindful breaks, we can enhance our efficiency and creativity.
- Practice: Begin your workday with a few minutes of mindful breathing. Throughout the day, take short breaks to stretch and breathe mindfully. When working on a task, give it your full attention, avoiding multitasking.
- In Relationships: Mindful communication and presence can strengthen our relationships. By listening deeply and responding thoughtfully, we can foster deeper connections and understanding.
- Practice: When interacting with others, practice active listening. Give them your full attention, making eye contact and acknowledging their words without interrupting. Respond with empathy and mindfulness.
- Self-Care: Mindful self-care involves taking time to nurture ourselves with awareness and intention. This can include activities like bathing, exercising, or simply relaxing.

- Practice: Treat yourself to a mindful self-care routine. For example, during a bath, notice the sensation of the water on your skin, the warmth, and the scent of any bath products. Engage fully with the experience, letting go of any distractions.

Overcoming Obstacles to Mindfulness Practice

Despite its benefits, maintaining a regular mindfulness practice can be challenging. Common obstacles include time constraints, restlessness, and self-doubt. Recognizing these challenges and developing strategies to overcome them is essential for sustaining mindfulness in everyday life.

1. Time Constraints: Finding time for mindfulness can be difficult in a busy schedule. However, even brief moments of mindfulness can be beneficial.
2. Strategy: Integrate mindfulness into daily activities, such as mindful breathing during a commute or mindful walking during a lunch break.
3. Restlessness: Restlessness and a busy mind can make it hard to focus during mindfulness practice. It's important to approach these moments with patience and compassion.
4. Strategy: Acknowledge restlessness without judgment and gently guide your focus back to the present moment. Using techniques like body scan or focusing on physical sensations can help ground your attention.
5. Self-Doubt: Doubts about the effectiveness of mindfulness or your ability to practice it can

undermine your efforts.
- Strategy: Remember that mindfulness is a practice, not a perfection. Be kind to yourself and recognize that every moment of awareness is valuable, regardless of how fleeting it may be.

The Benefits of Mindfulness

Physical and Mental Health Benefits
Mindfulness practice offers a wide range of physical and mental health benefits. Regular mindfulness meditation has been shown to lower blood pressure, enhance immune function, and reduce chronic pain. Mentally, it can decrease symptoms of anxiety, depression, and PTSD, contributing to overall emotional well-being.

Emotional Regulation and Stress Reduction
One of the most significant benefits of mindfulness is its ability to help us regulate our emotions. By observing our thoughts and feelings without becoming overwhelmed by them, we can respond to situations more calmly and thoughtfully. This emotional regulation leads to reduced stress and a greater sense of inner peace.

Enhanced Focus and Creativity
Mindfulness enhances our ability to concentrate and stay focused. By training our minds to remain in the present moment, we can improve our attention span and reduce distractions. Additionally, mindfulness can boost creativity by fostering a state of relaxed awareness,

where innovative ideas are more likely to emerge.

Mindfulness is a powerful tool for enhancing our well-being and deepening our connection to ourselves and the world around us. By understanding its principles, incorporating it into our daily routines, and overcoming common obstacles, we can experience its profound benefits. Embracing mindfulness allows us to live more fully in the present moment, cultivating a sense of peace, clarity, and joy in our lives.

Mindfulness Tip:
Practice the 5-4-3-2-1 Grounding Technique

Whenever you feel overwhelmed or distracted, use this simple exercise to bring yourself back to the present moment:

Notice 5 Things You Can See: Look around and name five things you can visually observe.
Notice 4 Things You Can Touch: Focus on textures around you—your clothing, a chair, or the ground beneath your feet.
Notice 3 Things You Can Hear: Tune into surrounding sounds, like birds, traffic, or even your own breath.
Notice 2 Things You Can Smell: Pay attention to scents, such as coffee, fresh air, or your perfume.
Notice 1 Thing You Can Taste: Focus on what's in your mouth or simply the sensation of your tongue.

This technique quickly grounds you and anchors your awareness in the present moment.

chapter 14

SOUND AND VIBRATION: FREQUENCIES FOR HEALING AND TRANSFORMATION

"IN THE SYMPHONY OF EXISTENCE, HEALING BEGINS WHEN YOU ALIGN WITH THE FREQUENCY OF YOUR TRUE SELF." – ZEN

The Science of Sound and Vibration

Sound is a powerful energy that travels through the air as waves, vibrating at different frequencies. These vibrations can influence the physical, emotional, and mental states of living beings. The human body, composed largely of water, is highly responsive to sound vibrations. Scientific studies have shown that sound can alter brainwave patterns, influence physiological processes, and affect our overall well-being.

Sound therapy, or the use of sound for healing purposes, has gained recognition in the scientific community. Different frequencies and types of sound can stimulate brainwave activity, promoting relaxation, focus, and emotional release. Binaural beats, for instance, are an example of how specific sound frequencies can entrain the brain, encouraging it to synchronize its wave patterns and achieve desired mental states.

Historical and Cultural Significance of Sacred Sounds

Throughout history, sacred sounds have played a significant role in various cultures and spiritual traditions. From the chanting of mantras in Hinduism and Buddhism to the use of singing bowls in Tibetan rituals, sound has been used as a tool for healing, meditation, and spiritual awakening.

In ancient Egypt, sound was believed to hold the power to heal and transform. The Greeks also recognized the therapeutic properties of music, with philosophers like Pythagoras studying the relationship between musical harmonics and the cosmos. Indigenous cultures around the world have long utilized sound in their rituals and ceremonies, understanding its ability to connect individuals with the divine and the natural world.

Exploring Different Sacred Sounds

Mantras and Chanting
Mantras are repetitive sounds or phrases that are chanted to aid concentration, invoke spiritual energies, and connect with higher states of consciousness. The syllable "Om," for example, is considered the primordial sound of the universe in Hinduism and Buddhism. Chanting "Om" is believed to align the practitioner with the vibration of the cosmos, fostering a sense of unity and peace.
Another common mantra is "So Hum," which translates to "I am That" in Sanskrit. This mantra is used to cultivate awareness of one's true nature and connection to the universal consciousness. By chanting mantras, practitioners can quiet the mind, focus their energy, and deepen their meditation practice.

Tibetan Singing Bowls and Gongs
Tibetan singing bowls and gongs are ancient instruments used in meditation, healing, and spiritual ceremonies. These instruments produce rich, resonant sounds that can induce deep relaxation and promote healing. When a singing bowl is struck or rubbed with a mallet, it produces a complex set of vibrations that create a harmonic resonance. This resonance can help balance the body's energy centers, or chakras, and

release physical and emotional blockages. Gongs, with their deep and powerful tones, are often used in sound baths to create an immersive soundscape that facilitates profound meditative experiences.

Nature Sounds and Their Calming Effects
Nature sounds, such as the rustling of leaves, the chirping of birds, or the sound of flowing water, have a soothing and grounding effect on the mind and body. These sounds connect us to the natural world and can evoke a sense of tranquility and well-being.
Listening to nature sounds can reduce stress, lower blood pressure, and improve mood. They can be used as a backdrop for meditation or relaxation practices, helping to create a peaceful and restorative environment.

Practicing with Sacred Sounds
Techniques for Using Sacred Sounds in Meditation
Incorporating sacred sounds into meditation can enhance the practice and deepen the experience. Here are some techniques to get started:
- Chanting Mantras: Choose a mantra that resonates with you, such as "Om" or "So Hum." Sit comfortably, close your eyes, and begin to chant the mantra slowly and rhythmically. Focus on the sound and vibration of the mantra, allowing it to anchor your awareness in the present moment.
- Listening to Singing Bowls: Find a recording of Tibetan singing bowls or use a bowl if you have one.

- Sit in a quiet space and listen to the sound of the bowl, allowing its vibrations to wash over you. Pay attention to the different tones and how they make you feel.
- Nature Sound Meditation: Use recordings of nature sounds, such as rain, ocean waves, or forest ambiance. Sit comfortably and listen to the sounds, imagining yourself in the natural environment. Let the sounds bring you into a state of relaxation and connection with nature.

Creating a Sacred Sound Practice at Home

Developing a regular sacred sound practice can be a powerful way to integrate these techniques into your daily life. Here are some steps to create your practice:

1. Set Up a Sacred Space: Designate a quiet and comfortable area in your home for your sound practice. Include items that inspire you, such as candles, crystals, or images.
2. Choose Your Instruments: Select the sacred sounds you want to work with, whether they are mantras, singing bowls, gongs, or nature recordings.
3. Establish a Routine: Set aside a specific time each day for your practice. Consistency is key to experiencing the benefits of sacred sound meditation.
4. Be Present: During your practice, focus on the sounds and your sensations. Allow yourself to be fully present, letting go of any distractions or thoughts.

Benefits of Sacred Sounds

Healing Properties of Sound
Sound has been used for centuries as a tool for healing. Different frequencies and vibrations can promote physical, emotional, and spiritual well-being. Sound therapy can reduce stress, alleviate pain, and improve overall health. The resonant tones of singing bowls and gongs can balance the body's energy centers and facilitate the release of tension and blockages.

Enhancing Meditation and Mindfulness with Sound
Incorporating sacred sounds into meditation can deepen the practice by providing a focal point for the mind. The vibrations of sound can induce a state of relaxation and inner peace, making it easier to achieve a meditative state. Sacred sounds can also enhance mindfulness by anchoring awareness in the present moment and fostering a sense of connection and harmony.

Connecting to Deeper Levels of Consciousness
Sacred sounds have the power to transport us to deeper levels of consciousness. By attuning to specific frequencies and vibrations, we can access states of heightened awareness and spiritual insight. Sound can act as a bridge between the physical and spiritual realms, facilitating experiences of oneness and transcendence.

Sound Frequencies

Different sound frequencies can have varying effects on the mind and body. For example, the frequency of 528 Hz, known as the "Love Frequency," is believed to promote healing and transformation. Other frequencies, such as 432 Hz and 741 Hz, are also associated with positive effects on consciousness and well-being. By working with these frequencies, we can harness the power of sound to support our spiritual growth and healing.

Main Sound Frequencies and Their Benefits
174 Hz - Pain Relief and Healing
- Benefits: This frequency is known to alleviate pain and reduce stress. It is often used in sound therapy to promote physical healing and relaxation.

285 Hz - Tissue Repair and Cellular Healing
- Benefits: This frequency is believed to support tissue and organ regeneration. It can help to rejuvenate and energize cells, promoting overall healing.

396 Hz - Liberating Guilt and Fear
- Benefits: This frequency helps to release feelings of guilt and fear. It is often used to clear negative emotions and promote a sense of liberation and inner peace.

417 Hz - Facilitating Change and Undoing Situations
- Benefits: This frequency is associated with facilitating change and undoing negative situations. It can help to clear past traumas and promote a fresh start.

528 Hz - DNA Repair and Transformation
- Benefits: Known as the "Love Frequency," 528 Hz is believed to promote DNA repair and transformation. It is associated with deep healing and positive transformation.

639 Hz - Enhancing Relationships and Connection
- Benefits: This frequency is used to improve communication, understanding, and harmony in relationships. It promotes a sense of connection and empathy.

741 Hz - Awakening Intuition and Consciousness
- Benefits: 741 Hz helps to awaken intuition and enhance spiritual consciousness. It is often used in meditative practices to promote inner wisdom and clarity.

852 Hz - Returning to Spiritual Order
- Benefits: This frequency is associated with returning to a spiritual order and alignment with higher consciousness. It helps to awaken inner strength and self-realization.

963 Hz - Activating Pineal Gland and Higher Consciousness
- Benefits: Known as the "Frequency of the Gods," 963 Hz is believed to activate the pineal gland and promote higher states of consciousness and spiritual enlightenment.

Additional Healing Frequencies

432 Hz - Natural Harmonization
- Benefits: This frequency is known for its natural harmonizing effects. It promotes a sense of peace and well-being, aligning with the natural rhythms of the universe.

111 Hz - Divine Connection
- Benefits: Often used in sacred spaces and rituals, 111 Hz is believed to facilitate divine connection and deep meditative states.

144 Hz - Balancing Energy
- Benefits: This frequency is associated with balancing energy fields and promoting equilibrium. It can help to restore harmony and balance in the body and mind.

These frequencies are used in various sound healing practices, such as listening to specific music, using tuning forks, singing bowls, and other sound therapy techniques. There are also unlimited resources online. Each frequency resonates with different aspects of the body and mind, offering unique healing properties and benefits.

The power of sacred sounds lies in their ability to influence our physical, emotional, and spiritual states. By exploring and incorporating mantras, singing bowls, gongs, and nature sounds into our practices, we can enhance our meditation, promote healing, and connect with deeper levels of consciousness. Sacred sounds offer a profound and transformative path to inner peace and spiritual awakening.

QUESTIONS FOR CONTEMPLATION

How do the sounds I surround myself with each day affect my mood, energy, and overall sense of well-being?

What frequencies or types of music resonate deeply with me, and how can I use them to support my healing and growth?

In moments of stillness, what vibrations can I feel within my body, and what messages might they carry about my current state of balance or imbalance?

How can I consciously incorporate sound and vibration into my daily life to create harmony and alignment with my higher self?

NOTES

chapter 15

CONNECTING WITH NATURE: RECLAIMING YOUR NATURAL WISDOM

"NATURE DOES NOT HURRY, YET EVERYTHING IS ACCOMPLISHED. ALIGN WITH ITS RHYTHM, AND WISDOM UNFOLDS." – ZEN

The Importance of Nature Connection

The Human-Nature Relationship

The bond between humans and nature is ancient and profound. Our ancestors lived in close harmony with the natural world, relying on its resources for survival and finding solace and inspiration in its beauty. Today, many of us live in urban environments, distanced from nature, which can lead to a sense of disconnection and imbalance.

Nature offers us a unique opportunity to reconnect with our roots and tap into a source of wisdom and healing that is always available. By understanding and nurturing our relationship with nature, we can enhance our physical, mental, and spiritual well-being.

Benefits of Spending Time in Nature

Spending time in nature has numerous benefits:
- Physical Health: Exposure to natural environments can lower blood pressure, reduce the risk of chronic diseases, and boost the immune system.
- Mental Health: Nature has a calming effect on the mind, reducing stress, anxiety, and depression. It enhances mood and promotes mental clarity.
- Spiritual Connection: Nature provides a space for reflection, inspiration, and a sense of oneness with the universe. It helps us connect to something greater than ourselves.

Mindfulness in Nature

Forest Bathing (Shinrin-yoku)
Forest bathing, or Shinrin-yoku, is a Japanese practice that involves immersing oneself in a forest environment to promote health and well-being. It is not about hiking or exercising but simply being present and taking in the forest atmosphere.
Practice: Find a quiet forest or wooded area. Walk slowly and mindfully, using all your senses to engage with your surroundings. Notice the sights, sounds, smells, and textures. Breathe deeply and allow yourself to relax and absorb the calming energy of the forest.

Mindful Hiking and Walking
Mindful hiking and walking involve bringing full awareness to the act of walking in nature. It combines physical activity with mindfulness, allowing us to connect deeply with the natural world.
Practice: Choose a nature trail or park. Walk at a comfortable pace, paying attention to each step. Notice the feeling of the ground beneath your feet, the rhythm of your breath, and the sounds around you. If your mind wanders, gently bring your focus back to the present moment.

Grounding and Earthing Practices
Grounding, or earthing, involves direct physical contact with the earth, which can help balance the body's energy and reduce inflammation.

Practice: Find a grassy area or beach. Remove your shoes and stand, walk, or sit with your bare feet on the ground. Focus on the sensations of the earth beneath you and visualize any stress or negativity being absorbed by the earth.

Nature-Based Activities for Awakening

Gardening and Its Therapeutic Effects
Gardening is a therapeutic activity that connects us to the cycles of nature and fosters a sense of nurturing and growth.
Practice: Start a small garden or care for a few potted plants. Engage in each task mindfully, whether it's planting seeds, watering, or weeding. Notice the changes and growth in your plants, reflecting on the parallels with your own personal growth.

Nature Journaling and Observation
Nature journaling involves recording observations, thoughts, and feelings about the natural world, enhancing our awareness and appreciation of nature's beauty and complexity.
Practice: Bring a journal and pen on your nature outings. Take time to observe your surroundings closely. Write or draw what you see, hear, and feel. Reflect on how these observations relate to your inner experiences.

Wildlife Watching and Eco-Therapy
Observing wildlife and engaging in eco-therapy can deepen our connection to nature and promote

emotional healing.

Practice: Find a quiet spot where you can observe birds, insects, or other wildlife. Sit quietly and watch their behaviors. Notice how being in their presence affects your mood and thoughts. Eco-therapy activities, such as guided nature walks and conservation projects, can also foster a deeper connection to the natural world.

Integrating Nature into Daily Life

Bringing Nature Indoors
Incorporating elements of nature into our living spaces can create a calming and restorative environment.
Practice: Add houseplants to your home or workspace. Use natural materials for decor, such as wood, stone, and shells. Play recordings of natural sounds, like flowing water or birdsong, to create a soothing atmosphere.

Creating a Nature-Inspired Mindfulness Space
Designing a mindfulness space inspired by nature can enhance your meditation and relaxation practices.
Practice: Choose a quiet corner of your home and decorate it with natural elements, such as plants, rocks, and driftwood. Use soft lighting and natural colors. Make this space a sanctuary where you can meditate, journal, or simply relax and connect with nature.

Regular Nature Retreats and Digital Detox
Taking regular breaks from technology and immersing yourself in nature can rejuvenate your mind and spirit.

Practice: Plan regular nature retreats, whether it's a weekend camping trip or a day hike. During these retreats, disconnect from digital devices to fully engage with the natural environment. Use this time to reflect, meditate, and recharge.

Reconnecting with nature is a powerful way to enhance our well-being and deepen our spiritual practice. By spending time in natural environments, practicing mindfulness in nature, and integrating nature into our daily lives, we can foster a greater sense of connection, peace, and harmony. Embrace the healing power of nature and allow it to guide you on your journey of awakening.

Tip: Focus on the sounds, smells, and textures around you to ground your energy

QUESTIONS FOR CONTEMPLATION

When was the last time I truly paused to observe and appreciate the natural world around me? What did I notice?

How does spending time in nature shift my energy, emotions, and perspective on life?

What lessons can I learn from the cycles and rhythms of nature, and how can I apply them to my own life?

In what ways can I deepen my connection with nature to align more fully with my inner wisdom and sense of purpose?

NOTES

chapter 16

SPIRITUAL PRACTICES FOR 5D LIVING

"SPIRITUAL PRACTICES ARE NOT ABOUT ESCAPING REALITY BUT EMBRACING IT WITH HIGHER AWARENESS AND UNCONDITIONAL LOVE."
– ZEN

Living in 5D consciousness is not just a state of mind; it is a way of being that permeates every aspect of life. It involves a deep alignment with love, compassion, and unity, creating a harmonious relationship with the self, others, and the universe. To sustain this higher state of consciousness, spiritual practices become essential. These practices help maintain a high vibration, foster deeper connection, and anchor the heart-centered qualities of 5D living.

One of the most powerful practices for sustaining 5D consciousness is meditation. Meditation quiets the mind, allowing you to access the stillness and peace within. It provides a space to connect with your higher self, receive guidance, and clear mental clutter that may cloud your awareness. While there are many forms of meditation, heart-centered meditation is particularly effective for 5D living. This practice involves focusing on the heart center, breathing into it, and cultivating feelings of love, compassion, and gratitude. By regularly tuning into the heart, you reinforce the 5D qualities of unconditional love and unity.

Breathwork is another transformative practice for maintaining a 5D state of being. Conscious breathing helps clear stagnant energy, release emotional blockages, and raise your vibrational frequency. Practices like pranayama, deep belly breathing, or coherent breathing not only bring clarity and calm but also create a deeper connection to your body and spirit.

In 5D living, breath becomes a bridge between the physical and the spiritual, allowing you to move energy through your body and align more easily with the flow of life.

Gratitude is a foundational practice for living in 5D. It is not just an emotion but a state of being that shifts focus from lack to abundance, from fear to love. Regularly expressing gratitude, whether through journaling, silent reflection, or sharing with others, raises your vibration and strengthens your connection to the heart. It helps you recognize the beauty in everyday moments, fostering a sense of joy and appreciation that aligns with the higher dimensions of consciousness. Gratitude also acts as a powerful magnet for more positive experiences, as it aligns your energy with the frequency of abundance.

Visualization is another key spiritual tool for 5D living. By using the mind's eye to imagine and feel the reality you wish to create, you align your energy with your intentions, making manifestation more fluid. Visualization is most effective when combined with elevated emotions like joy, love, and excitement. For example, visualizing yourself in a state of peace, joy, or abundance while feeling those emotions in your heart amplifies the manifestation process. This practice not only attracts desired outcomes but also reinforces the 5D principles of co-creation and empowerment. Spending time in nature is also an essential practice for anchoring 5D consciousness.

Nature embodies the qualities of peace, balance, and interconnectedness, offering a direct experience of unity with all living beings. Whether walking in the woods, sitting by the ocean, or simply observing a garden, nature has a grounding and healing effect on the spirit. It reminds you of the cyclical rhythms of life, encouraging a sense of trust and surrender to the flow of the universe. Nature meditation—where you consciously connect with the elements, listen to the sounds of the environment, and feel the energy of the earth—can deepen your sense of oneness and raise your vibration.

Acts of service are another vital aspect of 5D living. Serving others, whether through volunteer work, offering kindness, or sharing wisdom, reinforces the principle of unity. Service from a 5D perspective is not about obligation or sacrifice but about genuine love and compassion. It is an expression of the understanding that we are all connected, and that uplifting others also uplifts the self. By approaching service with a heart of love, you align more deeply with the essence of 5D consciousness.

Maintaining 5D consciousness is not about achieving a constant state of bliss but about cultivating practices that support your highest alignment. It is a process of ongoing refinement, where each practice, whether meditation, breathwork, gratitude, visualization, or service, contributes to a more stable and sustained experience of 5D living. The more you engage with these practices, the easier it becomes to embody the qualities of love, compassion, and unity, regardless of external circumstances.

Spiritual Practices

The Role of Gratitude and Compassion

Gratitude and compassion are foundational qualities that support spiritual growth and awakening. Practicing these virtues helps shift focus from ego-driven desires to a more heart-centered way of being.

Practice: Start a gratitude journal where you write down three things you are grateful for each day. Practice acts of kindness and compassion, both towards yourself and others. Reflect on how these practices influence your thoughts, emotions, and interactions.

Journaling and Self-Reflection

Journaling is a powerful tool for self-discovery and reflection. It allows you to explore your thoughts, emotions, and experiences, providing insights that can guide your spiritual journey.

Practice: Set aside time each day or week for journaling. Write about your experiences, thoughts, and feelings. Use prompts such as "What did I learn today?" or "How can I grow from this experience?" to deepen your self-reflection.

Creating Rituals and Ceremonies

Rituals and ceremonies provide a structured way to honor significant moments and transitions in life. They can be deeply personal and tailored to your spiritual beliefs and practices.

Practice: Create simple rituals to mark the beginning and end of each day, such as lighting a candle and setting intentions in the morning, and reflecting on your day in the evening. Design ceremonies for special occasions or milestones, incorporating elements that are meaningful to you, such as prayer, music, or symbolic objects.

Holistic approaches to awakening involve integrating various practices that nurture the mind, body, and spirit. By combining mindfulness, sound, nature, a conscious diet, movement, and spiritual practices, you can create a balanced and fulfilling path to personal growth and spiritual enlightenment. Embrace these practices with an open heart and mind, and allow them to guide you on your journey to awakening.

Affirmations for Gratitude

"I am deeply grateful for the abundance and blessings in my life, both big and small."

"With every breath, I cultivate a heart full of gratitude and joy."

"I choose to see the beauty and goodness in every moment, and I am thankful for all that I have."

QUESTIONS FOR CONTEMPLATION

Which spiritual practices resonate most with you, and how can you incorporate them more regularly into your life to support 5D living?

How do you currently use meditation or breathwork to connect with your higher self, and what changes have you noticed as a result?

Reflect on a recent moment of gratitude. How did this shift your perspective, and how can you cultivate more gratitude in your daily life?

What role does nature play in your spiritual journey? How can you deepen your connection to the earth as part of your 5D practice?

In what ways can you serve others from a place of love and unity, and how does this contribute to your own spiritual growth?

Notes

Chapter 17

LIVING IN 5D: TRANSFORMING YOUR RELATIONSHIPS, CAREER, AND DAILY LIFE

> "TO LIVE IN 5D IS TO SEE THE DIVINE IN ALL THINGS—YOUR WORK, YOUR RELATIONSHIPS, AND THE QUIET MOMENTS IN BETWEEN." – ZEN

As you evolve into 5D consciousness, the impact extends far beyond your internal world. Your relationships, career, and daily life begin to transform in profound ways. Living from a higher consciousness doesn't just change how you see yourself; it changes how you interact with others, how you approach your work, and how you engage with the world around you.

When you align with 5D, you live from the frequency of love and unity. You make decisions not from fear or ego but from a place of compassion and authenticity. This shift creates ripple effects that elevate your relationships, career, and everyday experiences. In this chapter, we'll explore how living in 5D can transform your external reality and bring more peace, purpose, and fulfillment into your life.

5D Relationships: Deepening Connections with Love

One of the most noticeable shifts in 5D consciousness is in your relationships. In 3D, relationships are often based on need, control, or attachment. Many people seek validation, approval, or security from others, leading to codependent or ego-driven dynamics. In contrast, 5D relationships are built on love, mutual respect, and a deep soul connection.

Living from the heart allows you to relate to others from a place of compassion and empathy. You no longer see relationships as transactions—what can I get from this person?—but as opportunities to grow, share, and support each other on your journeys. As you evolve, so do your connections, becoming more authentic and aligned with your true self.

Here are a few key aspects of 5D relationships:

- Unconditional Love: In 5D, love is no longer conditional on what someone does for you. You love others as they are, without trying to change or control them. You appreciate them for their unique essence, and you accept their journey as their own.
- Healthy Boundaries: While 5D relationships are based on love, they also involve clear boundaries. In 3D, you might have felt obligated to please others or put their needs ahead of your own. In 5D, you understand the importance of honoring your energy and creating healthy boundaries that allow for mutual respect and growth.
- Soul Connections: You may begin to attract soul connections—relationships that feel deeply aligned on a spiritual level. These connections often go beyond the surface, helping you evolve and expand. Soul connections can be romantic, platonic, or professional, and they bring a sense of purpose and growth to your life.

As you live more in 5D, you may find that some relationships naturally fall away. This is not a sign of failure, but a reflection of your growth. You are evolving into a higher version of yourself, and sometimes certain relationships that are based on old energies no longer resonate. Letting go with love and gratitude allows space for more aligned connections to enter your life.

5D Career: Aligning with Purpose

In 5D consciousness, your approach to work and career shifts dramatically. In 3D, many people pursue careers based on societal expectations, financial security, or ego-driven desires for status and success. In 5D, work becomes an extension of your soul's purpose. You seek not just to make a living but to make a difference—to contribute something meaningful to the world.

When you live in 5D, you start to align your career with your highest values, passions, and gifts. You no longer see work as a burden or something you "have to" do. Instead, work becomes an expression of your true essence, and you look for ways to serve others and the planet through your unique talents.

Here are a few ways living in 5D can transform your career:

- Purpose-Driven Work: You begin to prioritize work that aligns with your soul's purpose. This might mean shifting careers entirely or simply adjusting your current work to focus on what truly inspires you. In 5D, you are less concerned with how much money or status your work brings and more focused on how it aligns with your heart's calling.

- Flow and Ease: In 3D, work often feels like a constant struggle or hustle. In 5D, work flows more easily because you are aligned with your purpose. You attract opportunities that resonate with your higher self, and the right people, projects, and resources seem to appear at just the right time.
- Collaboration and Co-Creation: 5D consciousness is based on unity, so collaboration becomes a natural part of your work. You seek out partnerships and co-creations with like-minded individuals who share your vision and values. Working together to uplift each other and serve a higher purpose brings fulfillment and joy to your career.

If you're currently in a career that doesn't align with your soul's purpose, the shift to 5D consciousness may inspire you to make changes. This doesn't necessarily mean quitting your job overnight, but it may involve exploring new opportunities, passions, or creative outlets that feel more aligned with who you are becoming.

5D Daily Life: Living with Presence and Joy

Living in 5D also transforms your daily life in simple but profound ways. In 3D, life can feel rushed, stressful, and overwhelming, with a constant focus on achieving more or worrying about the future. In 5D, you learn to slow down and embrace the beauty of the present moment. You cultivate joy, peace, and gratitude in everyday experiences, no matter how small.

Here are a few ways 5D consciousness enhances your daily life:

• Mindful Presence: One of the gifts of 5D consciousness is the ability to be fully present in each moment. Whether you are drinking your morning coffee, going for a walk, or spending time with loved ones, you learn to appreciate the richness of the experience without rushing to the next task or worrying about the future.

• Gratitude for the Simple Things: In 5D, you develop a deep sense of gratitude for the simple pleasures of life. You no longer need extravagant experiences or constant stimulation to feel fulfilled. The sound of birds, the warmth of the sun, or a meaningful conversation can bring you immense joy and peace.

• Living in Alignment: In 3D, daily life often feels like a series of obligations or responsibilities. In 5D, you live in alignment with your soul, making choices that reflect your true desires and values. You prioritize self-care, rest, and activities that nourish your spirit, rather than simply doing what is expected of you.

• Surrender and Trust: One of the greatest shifts in 5D consciousness is the ability to surrender control and trust the flow of life. You no longer feel the need to force things to happen or worry about outcomes. Instead, you trust that the universe is always working in your favor and that everything is unfolding perfectly.

Challenges of Living in 5D

While living in 5D consciousness brings immense peace and fulfillment, it can also come with its own set of challenges, especially when navigating a world that is still largely rooted in 3D thinking. You may encounter moments where it feels difficult to stay in the higher vibration of 5D, especially when faced with negativity, conflict, or stress from the outside world.

Here are a few challenges you may experience in 5D, along with suggestions for how to navigate them:

- Maintaining Boundaries: As you live more from the heart, it's easy to become overly empathetic or take on the emotions of others. It's important to maintain clear boundaries and protect your energy, especially when dealing with people or situations that are rooted in fear or negativity.

- Staying Grounded: In 5D, you may feel more connected to your spiritual self, but it's important to stay grounded in your physical reality as well. Make time for grounding practices like walking in nature, physical exercise, or connecting with your body through mindfulness.

- Dealing with 3D Structures: You may still need to navigate 3D systems like work, finances, or societal expectations, even as you live from a 5D perspective. This can create tension at times, but remember that part of your journey is to bring the energy of love and unity into these structures. Stay patient and trust that you are contributing to the collective shift, even when it feels challenging.

Affirmations for 5D Living

"I live in alignment with unconditional love, unity, and infinite possibilities."

"Every thought, word, and action I choose reflects my highest self and serves the greater good."

"I embrace the flow of life, trusting the universe to guide me on my 5D journey."

QUESTIONS FOR CONTEMPLATION

How can I bring unconditional love and compassion into my daily interactions and relationships?

What aspects of my career or work bring me true joy and align with my higher purpose?

How can I infuse mindfulness and presence into the simple routines of my daily life?

What shifts in perspective would help me view challenges as opportunities for growth in a 5D reality?

Notes

chapter 18

Awakening Through Relationships

"Relationships are mirrors reflecting the truth of who we are, guiding us toward deeper understanding and growth."
− Zen

Relationships are one of the most potent catalysts for spiritual awakening and personal growth. Whether romantic, familial, or platonic, relationships reflect back aspects of yourself, offering profound insights into your strengths, weaknesses, and unhealed wounds. As mirrors of your inner world, they reveal your beliefs, patterns, and unconscious behaviors, creating opportunities for healing, transformation, and deeper alignment with your true self.

At the core of awakening through relationships is the concept of mirroring. The people you attract into your life often reflect qualities, patterns, or beliefs that you hold—both those you embrace and those you reject. For example, if you struggle with self-worth, you may attract partners or friends who mirror this insecurity by withholding love or validation. Conversely, if you are stepping into a more empowered version of yourself, you may attract people who reflect this growth, supporting and celebrating your journey.

Romantic relationships are particularly powerful in this regard, as they often trigger deep emotional responses that can bring unresolved wounds to the surface. These responses are not random but are invitations to heal aspects of yourself that have been hidden or denied. For example, feelings of jealousy or fear of abandonment often stem from past experiences or beliefs about worthiness and love. By exploring these triggers with compassion and curiosity, you can begin to heal the underlying wounds and create a more fulfilling relationship dynamic.

Soulmate and twin flame connections are two types of spiritual relationships that are believed to be catalysts for profound growth.

Soulmates are individuals with whom you have a deep soul connection, often involving lessons of love, compassion, and acceptance. While soulmate relationships can be harmonious and nurturing, they can also bring challenges that promote healing and evolution. Twin flames, on the other hand, are often described as two halves of the same soul, experiencing an intense and transformative connection. Twin flame relationships can be deeply spiritual, but they also tend to bring intense challenges, as they force individuals to confront their deepest fears, wounds, and unresolved karmic patterns. The purpose of these connections is to facilitate rapid spiritual growth, often involving a journey of separation and reunion that mirrors the process of inner healing and integration.

Boundaries play a critical role in awakening through relationships. Establishing healthy boundaries is not about building walls but about creating clear, compassionate limits that protect your energy and honor your needs. Healthy boundaries help maintain a balanced sense of self while allowing for meaningful connections with others. They prevent codependency, where one's sense of worth becomes entangled with another person's behavior or approval. By maintaining boundaries, you create a safe space for mutual growth, respect, and authentic communication.

Vulnerability is another essential element of awakening

through relationships. While it can be uncomfortable to expose your true feelings, fears, or desires, vulnerability fosters deeper intimacy and connection. It allows you to be seen and accepted as you are, creating a foundation of trust and authenticity. Vulnerability also encourages others to open up, creating a space for mutual healing and growth. When approached with openness and a willingness to grow, vulnerability can transform relationships into powerful spiritual journeys that mirror the path to self-realization.

Communication is the lifeblood of healthy, conscious relationships. Conscious communication involves not only expressing yourself honestly and clearly but also listening with empathy and understanding. It requires patience, compassion, and a willingness to resolve conflicts in a way that promotes growth rather than division. Techniques like nonviolent communication, active listening, and using "I" statements (e.g., "I feel…" rather than "You make me feel…") help create a space for dialogue that fosters mutual respect and deeper understanding.

Forgiveness is also crucial in relationships, serving as a tool for releasing resentment, guilt, and blame. Holding onto grudges or unresolved conflicts creates energetic blockages that hinder spiritual growth. Forgiveness, whether directed toward yourself or others, frees up energy, allowing for greater peace, compassion, and harmony. It does not mean condoning harmful behavior but rather letting go of the emotional weight it carries, creating space for healing and renewal.

Self-love is at the heart of all relationship dynamics. Without a strong foundation of self-love, relationships can become imbalanced, driven by neediness, validation-seeking, or fear of rejection. Cultivating self-love involves recognizing your worth, honoring your boundaries, and treating yourself with kindness and compassion. It is not about perfection but about embracing yourself fully, including your flaws and imperfections. As you strengthen self-love, you attract healthier, more fulfilling relationships that reflect this inner state of wholeness.

Awakening through relationships is not limited to romantic connections; it includes family dynamics, friendships, and even interactions with colleagues or strangers. Each relationship serves as a mirror, reflecting back different aspects of yourself and offering opportunities for growth. By approaching each interaction with openness, awareness, and a willingness to learn, you can transform relationships into pathways for spiritual evolution. Even challenging relationships hold lessons, as they often reveal areas where healing, forgiveness, or personal growth is needed.

The process of awakening through relationships ultimately leads to greater compassion, empathy, and unity. As you heal wounds, release judgments, and embrace vulnerability, you create a more authentic connection with others. This connection reflects a deeper sense of oneness, where relationships are no longer driven by ego or fear but by love, mutual growth, and spiritual alignment.

Conscious Relationships

Building Mindful and Compassionate Relationships
Conscious relationships are built on mindfulness, compassion, and mutual respect. These relationships enhance our emotional and spiritual well-being by fostering genuine connections and understanding.
Practice: Cultivate awareness in your interactions with others. Approach each relationship with an open heart and mind, and practice empathy and kindness.

Effective Communication and Active Listening
Effective communication is key to building and maintaining conscious relationships. It involves expressing yourself clearly and listening actively to others.
Practice: Use "I" statements to express your feelings and needs without blaming or criticizing others. Practice active listening by giving your full attention to the speaker, acknowledging their words, and responding thoughtfully. Avoid interrupting or planning your response while the other person is speaking.

Boundaries and Healthy Relationship Dynamics
Healthy relationships require clear boundaries and mutual respect. Setting and respecting boundaries helps maintain balance and prevent misunderstandings.
Practice: Communicate your boundaries clearly and respectfully. Be honest about your needs and limits, and respect the boundaries of others. Practice assertiveness without aggression, and strive for mutual understanding and compromise.

QUESTIONS FOR CONTEMPLATION

How do your current relationships mirror aspects of yourself, including both strengths and areas for growth?

What recurring patterns do you notice in your relationships, and how might they be linked to past wounds, beliefs, or karmic lessons?

How can you establish and maintain healthy boundaries that support both personal growth and meaningful connections with others?

What role does vulnerability play in your relationships, and how can you cultivate deeper intimacy through honest and open communication?

How can forgiveness, both for yourself and others, transform your relationships and create a more harmonious dynamic?

Notes

Chapter 19

SACRED FEMININE AND MASCULINE INTEGRATION

"TRUE HARMONY ARISES WHEN THE SACRED FEMININE AND MASCULINE UNITE, CREATING BALANCE WITHIN AND AROUND US."
– ZEN

Sacred feminine and masculine integration is an essential step in the journey of spiritual awakening. Every individual, regardless of gender, carries both feminine and masculine energies within them. These energies are not about traditional gender roles but represent fundamental aspects of consciousness that, when balanced and integrated, lead to greater wholeness, harmony, and alignment with the higher self. The sacred feminine is often associated with intuition, receptivity, nurturing, and creativity, while the sacred masculine embodies action, structure, protection, and focus. Both energies are vital for personal growth, as they complement and support each other.

The sacred feminine is the energy of flow, compassion, and connection. It is the intuitive, receptive part of the self that listens, feels, and nurtures. When the feminine energy is balanced, individuals are able to tap into their inner wisdom, embrace creativity, and foster deep emotional connections. This energy encourages slowing down, embracing stillness, and allowing life to unfold naturally. However, when the feminine is unbalanced or suppressed, it can manifest as passivity, indecisiveness, or a tendency to become overly emotional or dependent. Healing the sacred feminine involves practices that cultivate intuition, creativity, and self-nurturing. It requires embracing emotions without judgment, developing a strong connection to the body, and allowing oneself to receive love and support.

The sacred masculine, on the other hand, is the energy of action, discipline, and protection. It is the part of the self that sets goals, creates boundaries, and takes initiative. When the masculine energy is in balance, individuals feel confident, purposeful, and able to manifest their desires through focused action. The masculine energy encourages decisive action, assertiveness, and the ability to stand strong in one's truth. However, when the masculine is unbalanced or overemphasized, it can result in aggression, control, or rigid thinking. Healing the sacred masculine involves developing healthy boundaries, setting clear intentions, and taking inspired action. It also includes learning to protect and honor oneself and others without dominating or controlling situations.

Integration of the sacred feminine and masculine requires acknowledging both energies, embracing their qualities, and allowing them to coexist in harmony. This integration is not about diminishing one energy to elevate the other but about finding a balance that supports overall well-being. For example, the creative flow of the feminine can be grounded by the focus and discipline of the masculine, creating a productive yet joyful approach to life. Similarly, the action-oriented drive of the masculine can be guided by the intuition and compassion of the feminine, ensuring that decisions are aligned with the heart.

Healing and balancing these energies often start with self-awareness. Individuals need to identify which energy is more dominant and which may be underdeveloped. For instance, someone who struggles with setting boundaries or taking initiative may need to strengthen their masculine energy, while someone who finds it difficult to be vulnerable or receptive may need to cultivate their feminine energy. This awareness is key to creating a more balanced and integrated approach to life.

Meditation is a powerful tool for integrating the sacred feminine and masculine. During meditation, you can visualize the feminine energy as a gentle, nurturing light in the heart center, and the masculine energy as a strong, protective force around the body. Imagining these energies merging and harmonizing within the body can create a sense of inner unity. You can also use affirmations that honor both energies, such as, "I am both receptive and assertive," or, "I embrace my intuition and my ability to take action."

Creative expression is another way to balance these energies. Engaging in activities like painting, dancing, or writing can awaken the feminine, while goal-setting, strategic planning, or pursuing physical fitness can activate the masculine. By alternating between these activities or finding ways to blend them, you can create a dynamic balance that supports personal growth. For example, someone might journal their creative ideas (feminine) and then set specific goals to bring those ideas to life (masculine).

In relationships, the integration of the sacred feminine and masculine creates deeper harmony and mutual support. When both partners embrace their inner balance, they can relate to each other from a place of wholeness rather than dependency.

Communication becomes more open and empathetic (feminine), while boundaries are respected and commitments are honored (masculine). This balanced approach allows for authentic intimacy, as both partners feel seen, heard, and valued.

Balancing the sacred feminine and masculine is not only about personal growth but also about contributing to the collective shift toward unity consciousness. As more individuals embrace this integration, the collective consciousness moves away from outdated paradigms of dominance, competition, and control, evolving toward a more compassionate, cooperative, and harmonious world. This integration fosters greater equality, respect, and understanding, both within individuals and in relationships, communities, and societies.

QUESTIONS FOR CONTEMPLATION

Reflect on your own balance of feminine and masculine energies. Which energy feels more dominant, and which one do you feel needs more nurturing or development?

How can you cultivate a stronger connection to your sacred feminine through practices like creativity, meditation, or self-nurturing?

In what areas of your life can you strengthen your sacred masculine by setting boundaries, taking action, or creating structure?

How does the integration of these energies affect your relationships with others? Are there patterns of imbalance that you can address to create more harmonious interactions?

What affirmations or meditations can you use to honor both the sacred feminine and masculine within you, creating a sense of inner unity?

Notes

chapter 20

ENERGY HEALING MODALITIES

"ENERGY FLOWS WHERE ATTENTION GOES;
HEALING BEGINS WHEN WE ALIGN OUR
FOCUS WITH THE HARMONY WITHIN."
– ZEN

Energy healing encompasses a broad range of practices designed to cleanse, balance, and elevate the body's energy field, fostering physical, emotional, and spiritual well-being. While traditional energy healing methods like Reiki, chakra balancing, sound therapy, and crystal healing offer profound benefits, there are many other ways to enhance the healing process. These include nature connection, self-care, and practices that address both the energetic body and the physical self, creating a holistic approach to healing and transformation.

Nature Connection is one of the most accessible and effective ways to cleanse and elevate your energy. Nature itself is a powerful healer, as it vibrates at a high frequency and offers a direct experience of unity, grounding, and renewal. Simply spending time in nature—whether walking in the forest, sitting by a river, or feeling the sun's warmth—helps release negative energy and restore inner balance. Earthing, or walking barefoot on natural surfaces like grass or sand, is particularly effective for grounding energy and discharging electromagnetic pollution absorbed from modern environments. The earth's energy has a stabilizing effect, helping to calm the nervous system, reduce stress, and enhance mental clarity.

Self-care is another essential aspect of energy healing. While it is often associated with pampering or relaxation, true self-care involves practices that nurture the body, mind, and spirit. Physical self-care, such as regular exercise, proper nutrition, and adequate rest, supports the body's energy flow and overall vitality.

Mental self-care includes mindfulness practices, positive affirmations, and stress reduction techniques that clear mental clutter and promote a positive mindset.

Emotional self-care involves practices like journaling, expressing emotions, and engaging in creative activities that allow for emotional release and integration.

Spiritual self-care can involve meditation, prayer, or ritual, all of which help maintain a strong connection to your higher self and spiritual guides.

Grounding techniques play a crucial role in energy healing. Grounding helps anchor energy in the present moment, making it easier to release stress, anxiety, and energetic imbalances. Beyond earthing, other grounding methods include visualizing roots growing from the base of the spine into the earth, carrying grounding crystals like hematite or black tourmaline, or using grounding essential oils like cedarwood or vetiver. These techniques help stabilize energy, promote a sense of safety, and enhance emotional resilience.

Emotional Freedom Techniques (EFT) or tapping is a simple yet powerful energy healing method that involves tapping on specific meridian points while focusing on emotional distress or limiting beliefs. EFT combines the principles of acupressure and psychology, allowing individuals to release energy blockages, reduce anxiety, and transform negative thought patterns. It's a versatile practice that can be used to address everything from trauma and phobias to stress and self-limiting beliefs. By tapping on the body's energy meridians, EFT facilitates the flow of energy, promoting balance and emotional well-being.

Mindfulness and meditation are also fundamental energy healing practices. While meditation helps quiet the mind and connect with the higher self, mindfulness enhances awareness of the present moment, allowing individuals to observe their thoughts, emotions, and sensations without judgment. Mindfulness brings conscious awareness to the body's energy, making it easier to identify blockages, areas of tension, or unprocessed emotions. By cultivating a mindful approach to everyday life, individuals can maintain a higher vibration and respond to challenges with greater calm and clarity.

Bodywork therapies, such as massage, acupuncture, and reflexology, contribute to energy healing by addressing both the physical body and its energy pathways. Massage not only relaxes muscles but also stimulates energy flow, releasing tension and toxins from the body. Acupuncture, an ancient Chinese medicine practice, uses fine needles to activate specific points along the body's meridians, restoring energy balance and promoting healing. Reflexology, which involves applying pressure to specific points on the feet, hands, or ears, stimulates the body's energy pathways and supports overall well-being.
Energy-cleansing rituals can also support healing. Smudging with sage, palo santo, or other sacred herbs is a traditional practice used by many cultures to clear negative energy from a person, space, or object. The smoke from these herbs is believed to neutralize lower vibrations and purify the energy field.

Similarly, using salt baths or salt scrubs can clear energy blockages from the aura, promote relaxation, and cleanse the physical body. Regular energy-cleansing rituals help maintain a high vibration and support ongoing spiritual growth.

Sound healing, already mentioned, can also be expanded to include personal practices like vocal toning, chanting, or listening to binaural beats and solfeggio frequencies. Vocal toning involves using your own voice to produce sounds that resonate with different energy centers, promoting release and realignment. Chanting mantras, such as "Om" or "So Hum," can calm the mind and elevate the spirit. Listening to binaural beats and solfeggio frequencies helps shift brainwave patterns, facilitating states of relaxation, meditation, or creativity.

Lastly, creative expression can be a powerful form of energy healing. Whether through art, music, dance, or writing, creative activities allow for emotional release, insight, and alignment. Creativity is a form of energy that connects directly to the soul, making it an effective way to explore inner landscapes, process emotions, and express the unspoken aspects of the self. Engaging in creative pursuits not only heals but also raises vibration, promoting joy, passion, and a sense of fulfillment.

By integrating these diverse energy healing modalities into your spiritual practice, you can create a holistic approach that addresses all levels of your being—physical, emotional, mental, and spiritual. Each practice offers unique benefits, contributing to a higher vibration, clearer energy flow, and deeper spiritual connection.

As you explore and personalize your energy healing journey, you will find a combination of methods that resonate most deeply with your essence, supporting your evolution toward a more balanced, aligned, and awakened state of consciousness.

Combining Mindfulness, Sound, and Nature

Integrating Practices for a Holistic Awakening
Combining mindfulness, sound, and nature practices can create a powerful synergy that enhances overall well-being and accelerates spiritual awakening. Each practice complements the others, providing a comprehensive approach to balancing mind, body, and spirit.
Practice: Begin your day with a mindfulness meditation to center yourself. Incorporate sacred sounds, such as chanting or listening to singing bowls, to deepen your practice. Spend time in nature daily, even if it's just a short walk, to ground yourself and connect with the natural world.

Developing a Personalized Routine
Creating a routine that integrates these practices can help maintain consistency and ensure that you are nurturing all aspects of your being.
Practice: Design a daily or weekly schedule that includes time for mindfulness meditation, sacred sound sessions, and nature connection. Customize this routine to fit your lifestyle and preferences, making adjustments as needed to stay aligned with your goals.

Diet and Consciousness

Foods That Support Higher Consciousness

The food we consume can significantly impact our physical and spiritual well-being. A diet rich in whole, natural foods supports higher consciousness by providing the necessary nutrients for optimal brain function and energy levels.

Practice: Focus on a plant-based diet that includes fresh fruits, vegetables, whole grains, nuts, seeds, and legumes. Avoid processed foods, excessive sugar, and artificial additives. Incorporate superfoods like spirulina, chia seeds, and goji berries to boost nutrient intake.

Mindful Eating Practices

Mindful eating involves paying full attention to the eating experience, from the selection and preparation of food to the act of eating and the sensations that follow.

Practice: Before eating, take a moment to express gratitude for your food. Eat slowly, savoring each bite, and paying attention to the flavors, textures, and smells. Notice how the food makes you feel, both physically and emotionally. Avoid distractions such as television or smartphones during meals.

Movement and Energy Flow

Yoga and Its Benefits for Awakening

Yoga is a practice that unites the mind, body, and spirit through physical postures, breath control, and meditation. It promotes flexibility, strength, and inner

peace, making it a powerful tool for awakening.
Practice: Incorporate a daily or weekly yoga routine that includes a mix of asanas (postures), pranayama (breathwork), and meditation. Focus on poses that open the heart and balance the chakras, such as the warrior series, tree pose, and child's pose.

Qi Gong and Tai Chi Practices
Qi Gong and Tai Chi are ancient Chinese practices that cultivate the body's vital energy, or "qi." These gentle, flowing movements enhance physical health, mental clarity, and spiritual awareness.
Practice: Dedicate time each day to practice Qi Gong or Tai Chi. Start with basic exercises that focus on breath control and slow, deliberate movements. As you become more comfortable, explore more advanced sequences that promote energy flow and balance.

TIP: Quick Breathing Exercise, Inhale for a count of 4, hold for 4, and exhale for 6. This helps calm the mind and balance energy.

QUESTIONS FOR CONTEMPLATION

What energy healing practices have you tried so far, and which ones resonate most with you? How can you incorporate them more consistently into your routine?

Reflect on your self-care habits. Are there areas—physical, mental, emotional, or spiritual—that need more attention or balance?

How does spending time in nature affect your energy and mood, and what regular practices can you establish to connect more deeply with the natural world?

What forms of creative expression bring you the most joy and healing? How can you integrate more creativity into your spiritual journey?

How can you use energy-cleansing rituals, like smudging or salt baths, to maintain a high vibration and support ongoing healing?

Notes

Part 4

Advanced Exploration of Consciousness

chapter 21

INTUITION AND PSYCHIC DEVELOPMENT

*"INTUITION IS THE VOICE OF YOUR SOUL;
PSYCHIC DEVELOPMENT IS LEARNING TO
TRUST ITS QUIET WISDOM."
– ZEN*

Intuition and psychic development are integral aspects of the journey toward awakening higher consciousness. Intuition is the inner knowing that goes beyond rational thought, offering insights, guidance, and clarity that often cannot be explained logically. It is the voice of the higher self, gently directing you toward alignment with your soul's purpose. Psychic development takes intuition a step further, opening doors to spiritual gifts like clairvoyance, telepathy, or energy reading. Both intuition and psychic abilities can be cultivated through dedicated practice, allowing for deeper spiritual awareness and more harmonious living.

Intuition is often described as a "gut feeling," an inner sense of what feels right or wrong. It is a natural part of everyone's consciousness, but societal conditioning, fear, and overreliance on logic often dull this inner voice. As individuals progress on their spiritual journey, they begin to recognize the value of intuition as a reliable guide. This recognition involves listening to subtle signals—physical sensations, emotional responses, or sudden insights—that arise when faced with decisions or situations. Honoring these signals, even when they conflict with logical reasoning, helps strengthen trust in intuitive guidance.

Psychic development involves the activation of spiritual senses beyond the five physical senses. These spiritual senses, often referred to as the "clairs," include clairvoyance (clear seeing), clairaudience (clear hearing), clairsentience (clear feeling), and claircognizance (clear knowing). Each person has unique psychic abilities that can be awakened through practice and openness. For example, some may find that they have vivid visual impressions (clairvoyance), while others may hear messages in the form of inner words or sounds (clairaudience). Developing these abilities requires patience, consistent practice, and a willingness to explore different methods.

Meditation is a foundational practice for developing both intuition and psychic abilities. By quieting the mind, meditation creates space for intuitive insights and spiritual messages to emerge. A specific form of meditation, known as "third-eye meditation," involves focusing awareness on the area between the eyebrows, often referred to as the "third eye" or the sixth chakra. This chakra is associated with inner vision, higher perception, and spiritual insight. Regular meditation on this chakra can enhance clairvoyant abilities, deepen intuitive awareness, and facilitate clearer spiritual communication.

Dreamwork is another effective tool for strengthening intuition and psychic development. Dreams often serve as a bridge between the conscious and subconscious mind, offering symbolic messages and guidance from the higher self or spiritual guides. Keeping a dream journal helps capture details, patterns, and themes that might otherwise be forgotten. By reflecting on dream content, individuals can uncover hidden messages, receive insights about unresolved issues, and even predict future events. Lucid dreaming, where the dreamer becomes aware that they are dreaming and can consciously interact with the dream, is another aspect of psychic development that can be explored.

Another important practice is energy sensing, which involves becoming attuned to the energies of people, places, or objects. This practice enhances clairsentience, the ability to sense energy through feelings and sensations. To develop energy sensing, individuals can begin by focusing on their physical and emotional responses when entering a room, meeting someone new, or handling an object. The goal is to become aware of subtle energetic shifts, such as feeling lighter or heavier, warmer or cooler, more comfortable or uneasy. By tuning into these sensations, individuals can gain valuable information about the energy around them.

Telepathy, the ability to send and receive thoughts without verbal communication, is another aspect of psychic development. While often seen as a rare or mystical gift, telepathy is actually a natural extension of deep intuitive awareness. To cultivate telepathy, individuals can practice sending simple thoughts or images to a willing partner and then receiving feedback about what was perceived. This practice requires a quiet mind, focused intention, and trust in the process. Over time, telepathy can become a useful tool for enhancing communication and understanding, especially in close relationships.

Psychometry is the ability to read the energy of an object by holding it and tuning into its history or the emotions associated with it. This psychic skill is based on the idea that objects absorb and retain energy from the people and events they come into contact with.

To practice psychometry, individuals can start by holding an object, such as a piece of jewelry or a personal item, and allowing impressions, images, or emotions to arise. While the information received may not always be clear at first, regular practice can sharpen this ability.

Working with spirit guides and angels can also support intuition and psychic development. Spirit guides are non-physical beings who offer guidance, protection, and support on the spiritual journey. To connect with spirit guides, individuals can use guided meditations, set intentions to receive messages, or ask for signs in daily life. These signs may appear as repeated numbers, symbols, or messages that offer clarity and confirmation. Building a relationship with spirit guides involves trust, patience, and consistent communication, often through prayer, meditation, or journaling.

Intuition and psychic development also benefit from grounding practices, as they ensure that individuals remain centered and balanced while exploring higher realms of perception. Grounding can be achieved through practices like earthing, mindful breathing, or using grounding crystals like hematite or black tourmaline. By staying grounded, individuals can prevent energetic overwhelm, maintain clarity, and integrate spiritual insights more effectively.

Developing intuition and psychic abilities is not about gaining power or control but about deepening the connection to the higher self and the universe. It is a path of spiritual exploration that requires openness, humility, and a commitment to growth. As individuals enhance their intuitive and psychic abilities, they become more aligned with their soul's purpose, making choices that reflect their highest truth.

Affirmations for Intuition

"I trust my inner wisdom to guide me with clarity and confidence."

"My intuition is a powerful compass that always leads me to the highest good."

"I am deeply connected to my inner voice and the truth it reveals."

"With each decision, I align more fully with my intuitive knowing."

"I honor and nurture my intuition as a sacred gift within me."

QUESTIONS FOR CONTEMPLATION

How do you currently experience intuition, and what steps can you take to strengthen your trust in this inner guidance?

Which psychic abilities are you most drawn to, and how can you begin exploring them in a practical and safe way?

Reflect on a recent intuitive insight or "gut feeling" you had. How did you respond to it, and what was the outcome?

How can practices like meditation, dreamwork, or energy sensing support your psychic development, and which ones resonate with you the most?

What role do spirit guides or angels play in your spiritual journey, and how can you deepen your connection with them for greater guidance and support?

NOTES

chapter 22

KUNDALINI AWAKENING: UNLOCKING THE ENERGY WITHIN

"KUNDALINI IS THE DORMANT SPARK WITHIN, IGNITING THE JOURNEY TOWARD PROFOUND TRANSFORMATION AND DIVINE CONNECTION."
— ZEN

Kundalini awakening is one of the most powerful and transformative experiences on the journey of spiritual evolution. Often described as a spiritual "rebirth," it involves the activation of dormant spiritual energy at the base of the spine, often symbolized as a coiled serpent. When this energy awakens, it travels up through the chakras, purifying and expanding awareness at each level. This process can lead to profound physical, emotional, mental, and spiritual changes, catalyzing a deeper connection to one's higher self and the universe.

The term "Kundalini" originates from ancient Sanskrit texts, where it is depicted as a primal life force that lies coiled at the base of the spine, waiting to be awakened. In its dormant state, Kundalini energy remains latent, sustaining the body's basic functions but not fully activated. Once awakened, however, this energy rises through the Sushumna, the central energy channel that runs along the spine, passing through the seven major chakras. As it rises, Kundalini clears energy blockages, releases repressed emotions, and enhances spiritual perception.

A Kundalini awakening can be spontaneous or intentional. Spontaneous awakenings often occur unexpectedly, triggered by deep meditation, spiritual practices, trauma, or even a significant life event. These awakenings can be intense and overwhelming, as the energy surges through the body, bringing suppressed emotions, traumas, or memories to the surface for healing. Intentional awakenings, on the other hand, are usually pursued through practices like Kundalini yoga, breathwork, or meditation. These practices aim to awaken the energy gradually, allowing for a more controlled and integrated experience.

The experience of Kundalini awakening varies widely from person to person, depending on their energy, spiritual readiness, and state of mind. Common sensations during an awakening include heat or warmth along the spine, tingling in the body, spontaneous movements (known as Kriyas), and feelings of bliss or ecstasy. Some individuals may also experience visions, heightened intuition, or spontaneous spiritual insights as the energy activates the higher chakras, especially the third eye and crown. While these sensations can be exhilarating, they can also be unsettling, particularly if the individual is unprepared or unaware of what is happening.

The Kundalini process is not solely physical; it involves deep emotional and mental purification. As the energy rises, it pushes unresolved traumas, fears, and limiting beliefs to the surface, demanding attention and healing. This phase can be challenging, as it often brings about a "dark night of the soul," a period of confusion, existential questioning, and emotional upheaval. However, this purification is essential for clearing the way for greater spiritual awareness and a higher vibrational state. By embracing these challenges with compassion and a willingness to let go of old patterns, individuals can move through this phase and emerge stronger, clearer, and more aligned.

To support Kundalini awakening, it is crucial to maintain a regular spiritual practice that grounds and balances the energy. Kundalini yoga is one of the most effective practices, as it combines physical postures, breathwork, mantra chanting, and meditation to awaken and direct the energy. The practice helps strengthen the nervous system, open the chakras, and prepare the body to handle the intensity of the awakened Kundalini. Pranayama, or controlled breathing, is particularly beneficial, as it channels energy through the body, calms the mind, and enhances focus.

Meditation is another essential tool for navigating Kundalini awakening. By quieting the mind, meditation allows for a clearer connection to the higher self and spiritual guidance. Third-eye meditation, focusing on the space between the eyebrows, can help activate clairvoyant abilities and deepen spiritual insights. Grounding meditations, which involve visualizing roots extending from the body into the earth, help stabilize the energy, reduce anxiety, and promote inner peace.

Nutrition and lifestyle play a significant role in supporting Kundalini awakening. A clean, balanced diet rich in fresh fruits, vegetables, and whole foods can enhance the body's capacity to handle the energetic shifts associated with the awakening process. Staying hydrated is also important, as water helps regulate energy flow and flush toxins from the body. In addition, practices like spending time in nature, earthing, and engaging in light physical activities like walking or gentle yoga can help ground the energy and promote balance.

While Kundalini awakening can be transformative, it is essential to approach it with respect and caution. The energy can be intense, and if not properly managed, it can lead to physical discomfort, emotional instability, or mental confusion. This is why it is recommended to work with an experienced teacher, healer, or spiritual guide who can offer support, guidance, and techniques to help integrate the experience. Having a strong support network, including friends, mentors, or spiritual communities, can also be invaluable during this process. The ultimate purpose of Kundalini awakening is spiritual liberation and self-realization. As the energy moves through the body, it dissolves the illusion of separation, allowing for a direct experience of unity consciousness. Individuals often describe a sense of oneness with all life, heightened compassion, and a profound sense of inner peace. While the awakening journey can be challenging, it leads to a greater alignment with one's soul, a deeper understanding of life's mysteries, and an expanded sense of purpose.

QUESTIONS FOR CONTEMPLATION

Have you experienced any sensations, emotions, or visions that you believe may be related to Kundalini awakening? How did you respond to these experiences?

What practices, such as Kundalini yoga, breathwork, or meditation, resonate with you as tools for safely awakening and managing this energy?

How do you handle the emotional and mental challenges that arise during your spiritual journey? Are there specific tools or techniques that help you stay balanced?

In what ways can grounding practices, like spending time in nature or earthing, support your journey with Kundalini energy?

How can you cultivate a sense of trust in the Kundalini process, embracing both the intense energy and the deep transformation it brings?

Notes

Chapter 23

QUANTUM CONSCIOUSNESS: EXPLORING INFINITE POSSIBILITIES

"QUANTUM CONSCIOUSNESS REVEALS THE INFINITE POSSIBILITIES WITHIN, WHERE REALITY BENDS TO THE POWER OF AWARENESS."
– ZEN

Quantum consciousness is a profound aspect of awakening that bridges the realms of spirituality and science. It offers a deeper understanding of the interconnected nature of reality, where everything is energy and consciousness is the fundamental force that shapes the universe. Unlike the linear, cause-and-effect thinking of 3D reality, quantum consciousness embraces the idea that multiple possibilities exist simultaneously, influenced by intention, observation, and vibrational frequency. This perspective opens up new avenues for personal transformation, co-creation, and spiritual expansion.

At its core, quantum consciousness is based on the principles of quantum physics, which reveal that matter is not solid but consists of energy waves that respond to observation. The famous "observer effect" in quantum mechanics suggests that the mere act of observing a particle changes its state. This principle extends beyond particles to the realm of human consciousness, implying that your thoughts, intentions, and beliefs influence the reality you experience. In other words, reality is not fixed but fluid, shaped by the energy you emit and the focus of your awareness.

In practical terms, quantum consciousness invites you to see yourself as both a creator and a participant in the unfolding of reality. This shift in perspective moves you from a mindset of limitation to one of possibility. It encourages you to explore the idea that every thought, emotion, and intention carries a frequency that interacts with the quantum field, a vast network of energy that connects everything in existence. By aligning your frequency with higher states of consciousness, such as love, gratitude, or joy, you can influence the quantum field to manifest desired outcomes.

One of the most powerful aspects of quantum consciousness is the understanding of non-locality, the idea that energy and information are not confined to one location but are interconnected across space and time. This concept aligns with spiritual teachings that emphasize unity and oneness, suggesting that separation is an illusion. Non-locality also implies that changes made at the level of consciousness—such as healing past wounds, shifting beliefs, or raising your vibration—can have far-reaching effects on your reality and the collective consciousness.

Parallel realities and multiple timelines are other intriguing aspects of quantum consciousness. This perspective suggests that every choice . full bookyou make creates a new timeline, leading to different potential outcomes. In this way, the universe is seen as a multiverse, with countless parallel realities existing simultaneously. You have the ability to shift between these realities by changing your beliefs, intentions, and frequency. For example, by focusing on a reality where you are thriving, healthy, and aligned with your purpose, you can draw that version of reality closer, making it more probable.

Quantum consciousness also emphasizes the power of the present moment. Since the quantum field responds to current vibrations, the energy you emit now determines your future experiences. This understanding underscores the importance of mindfulness and presence, as they allow you to consciously shape your reality from moment to moment. Practices like meditation, gratitude, and affirmations help maintain a high vibration, aligning you with desired outcomes in the quantum field. Visualization is a potent tool for accessing quantum consciousness. By vividly imagining your desired reality as if it already exists, you communicate with the quantum field, sending out a clear signal that aligns with that reality. The more detailed and emotionally charged your visualization, the stronger the influence on the quantum field. For example, if you wish to manifest a fulfilling relationship, visualize not only the physical aspects but also the emotional connection, joy, and harmony you seek. By embodying the feelings associated with this reality, you align your energy with it, making it more likely to manifest.

The law of resonance is another principle that aligns with quantum consciousness. This law states that similar frequencies attract each other, much like a tuning fork causing another to vibrate at the same pitch. In terms of consciousness, this means that your inner state attracts corresponding experiences in the external world. If you resonate with abundance, you attract abundance; if you resonate with fear, you attract experiences that validate fear. By becoming aware of your dominant frequencies, you can consciously shift them to align with what you wish to experience. Intuition and synchronicity are heightened within the realm of quantum consciousness. As you raise your vibration and align with higher states of awareness, you become more attuned to the subtle signals of the universe. Intuition becomes a reliable guide, offering insights that bypass the logical mind, while synchronicities act as confirmation that you are aligned with the quantum field. These synchronicities, often seen as "meaningful coincidences," reinforce your connection to the flow of life and the unfolding of your intentions.

Healing through quantum consciousness is also possible, as it involves working with energy and intention at a fundamental level. Practices like energy healing, visualization, and sound therapy can shift energy patterns within the body, creating changes that resonate at the quantum level. For example, visualizing light filling an area of pain or imbalance can initiate energetic changes that support physical healing. Similarly, affirmations that focus on wellness, such as "Every cell in my body vibrates with health," send powerful signals to the quantum field, promoting healing and transformation.

Ultimately, quantum consciousness is about embracing your role as a co-creator of reality. It invites you to explore the vast potential of your mind, spirit, and energy, using your intentions, beliefs, and emotions to shape your experiences. This level of awareness fosters greater responsibility, as you recognize that your inner state not only affects your own life but also contributes to the collective consciousness. As you align with quantum principles, you open yourself to infinite possibilities, where limitations dissolve, and spiritual growth accelerates.

Affirmations for Healing

"My body, mind, and spirit are in harmony, and I welcome complete healing into my life."

"I release all that no longer serves me and make space for renewal and wholeness."

"Every breath I take fills me with peace, strength, and healing energy."

"I trust the natural flow of life to guide me toward balance and well-being."

"I am worthy of healing, love, and the full expression of my true self."

QUESTIONS FOR CONTEMPLATION

How do your thoughts, beliefs, and emotions shape your current reality? What changes can you make to align more closely with your desired outcomes?

What role does non-locality play in your understanding of unity and oneness, and how can this perspective enhance your relationships with others?

How can visualization and the law of resonance support your manifesting and co-creation efforts within the quantum field?

Reflect on a recent synchronicity you experienced. What message or confirmation did it offer about your current path?

How can you use mindfulness and presence to create positive shifts in the quantum field, influencing your reality moment by moment?

Notes

chapter 24

MANIFESTING AND CO-CREATION

"MANIFESTATION BEGINS WHERE INTENTION ALIGNS WITH BELIEF, AND CO-CREATION FLOURISHES IN THE ENERGY OF TRUST AND ACTION."
– ZEN

Manifesting and co-creation are central to the journey of awakening consciousness. They involve the realization that individuals are not passive participants in life but active creators of their reality. Through the conscious use of thoughts, emotions, beliefs, and intentions, individuals can shape their experiences and align with their soul's purpose. Manifesting is the process of turning desires into reality through focused intention and energy alignment, while co-creation emphasizes the collaborative aspect of creating with the universe, spirit guides, or a higher power.

At its core, manifesting begins with clarity of desire. It requires a deep understanding of what you truly want, not just on a superficial level but from the heart. This clarity comes from self-reflection and connecting with your inner self to identify desires that align with your values and spiritual purpose. Desires rooted in ego or fear often lead to temporary fulfillment, while desires that resonate with the higher self create lasting joy, peace, and alignment. Once clear about your desires, it's important to set specific, positive intentions. For example, rather than setting an intention to "avoid failure," reframe it as "achieve success in alignment with my soul's purpose."

The next step in manifesting is to align your thoughts, emotions, and energy with your desires. This alignment is crucial because the universe responds not just to what you want, but to the energy you radiate. If your thoughts are focused on lack, fear, or doubt, you may inadvertently attract experiences that reflect these vibrations. To shift into a more positive frequency, it's helpful to use affirmations, visualizations, and gratitude. Visualizing your desired reality as if it has already manifested is a powerful way to create energetic alignment. By feeling the emotions associated with this reality—joy, love, peace—you amplify the attraction process.

Belief is a key element in manifesting. It's not enough to simply desire something; you must also believe that it is possible and that you are worthy of receiving it. Limiting beliefs, such as "I don't deserve success" or "It's too good to be true," can block the manifestation process, even if intentions are strong. Identifying and transforming these beliefs is essential for successful manifesting. This transformation often involves using affirmations, EFT (Emotional Freedom Techniques), or subconscious reprogramming to replace limiting beliefs with empowering ones. For example, you might replace "I'm not good enough" with "I am worthy of all the abundance the universe has to offer."

Co-creation takes manifesting to a higher level, emphasizing collaboration with the universe or higher consciousness. Co-creation is based on the understanding that while you have free will to set intentions and take action, there is also a divine timing and flow that guides the process. It involves surrendering control over how and when manifestations will unfold, trusting that the universe has a plan that serves your highest good. This requires a balance between inspired action and letting go—taking steps toward your goals while allowing space for unexpected opportunities, signs, and synchronicities.

Gratitude is a powerful tool in both manifesting and co-creation. It not only raises your vibration but also signals to the universe that you are open to receiving more. Expressing gratitude for what you already have, as well as for what you are manifesting (even before it arrives), creates a magnetic energy that attracts more of the same. Daily gratitude practices, whether through journaling, meditation, or simply offering thanks, help keep your energy aligned with abundance and joy.

Taking inspired action is a crucial aspect of manifesting. While thoughts, emotions, and energy are powerful, they must be accompanied by tangible steps toward your goals. Inspired action differs from forced or purely logical action in that it arises from intuition, excitement, or a sense of flow. It often feels effortless, as it is guided by the higher self or spiritual guidance. For example, you might feel a sudden urge to call someone, attend an event, or start a new project—these impulses are often aligned with the path of co-creation.

Visualization is one of the most effective techniques for manifesting. By vividly imagining your desired outcome, you create a mental blueprint that guides your energy and intentions. Visualization can be enhanced by adding sensory details—imagining the sights, sounds, smells, and feelings associated with the manifested reality. For example, if you are visualizing a new home, imagine the colors of the walls, the scent of fresh flowers in the kitchen, and the feeling of comfort and security. The more detailed and emotionally charged the visualization, the stronger the energy it generates. Manifesting also benefits from the use of tools like vision boards, affirmations, and mantras. Vision boards are visual representations of your desires, created from images, words, and symbols that resonate with your intentions. By placing the vision board in a visible location and engaging with it regularly, you reinforce your focus and motivation. Affirmations and mantras serve as reminders of your goals and help reprogram the subconscious mind, replacing limiting beliefs with empowering ones.

It's important to understand that not every desire will manifest exactly as envisioned. Sometimes, what you manifest may come in a different form, or it may arrive later than expected. This is part of the co-creation process, where the universe delivers what is truly aligned with your highest good. It's essential to approach manifesting with a sense of detachment, trusting that the universe will bring what is needed at the right time. This detachment allows for greater flexibility, resilience, and openness to unexpected blessings.

The process of manifesting and co-creation is deeply empowering, as it aligns you with your innate creative potential. It shifts your mindset from victimhood to mastery, helping you recognize that you have the power to shape your reality through conscious intention, belief, and action. It also fosters a deeper relationship with the universe, as you learn to trust its guidance, timing, and wisdom.

QUESTIONS FOR CONTEMPLATION

What desires feel most aligned with your soul's purpose, and how can you set clear, specific intentions to manifest them?

How can you shift your thoughts and emotions to match the frequency of what you want to attract?

Reflect on a past manifestation. What beliefs or actions contributed to its success, and how can you apply these insights to your current goals?

How can you balance inspired action with surrender, trusting that the universe will guide you toward your highest good?

What daily practices, such as gratitude, visualization, or affirmations, can you use to enhance your manifesting and co-creation process?

Notes

chapter 25

ADVANCED PRACTICES FOR DEEPENING CONSCIOUSNESS

"THE DEPTH OF YOUR CONSCIOUSNESS IS NOT MEASURED BY HOW MUCH YOU KNOW, BUT BY HOW MUCH YOU LET GO." – ZEN

Introduction to Altered States

Altered states of consciousness are conditions in which the mind experiences a shift from its usual waking state. These states can provide profound insights and transformative experiences. Common altered states include lucid dreaming, astral projection, and deep meditative states.

- **Lucid Dreaming:** A lucid dream is a dream in which the dreamer is aware that they are dreaming. This awareness allows them to control aspects of the dream, explore the subconscious mind, and overcome fears.
- **Astral Projection:** Astral projection, or out-of-body experiences (OBEs), involves the sensation of leaving the physical body and traveling in a non-physical form. This practice can offer insights into the nature of consciousness and the afterlife.
- **Deep Meditation:** Advanced meditation techniques can induce altered states of consciousness, such as a sense of timelessness, unity with the universe, and profound inner peace.

Safe Practices for Exploring Altered States

Exploring altered states requires caution and preparation to ensure safety and meaningful experiences.

Practice:

Preparation: Educate yourself about the practice you wish to explore. Read books, attend workshops, and seek guidance from experienced practitioners.

Set and Setting: Ensure a safe and comfortable environment. Your mental state and physical surroundings significantly impact the experience.
Intentions: Set clear and positive intentions before attempting to enter an altered state. This helps guide the experience and ensures a constructive outcome.
Grounding Techniques: Learn grounding techniques to safely return to your normal waking state. Techniques such as focusing on your breath, physical sensations, or repeating a grounding mantra can be effective.

Mystical and Esoteric Practices

Introduction to Astrology and Its Influence on Consciousness
Astrology is the study of the movements and relative positions of celestial bodies and their influence on human affairs and natural phenomena. Many believe that the positions of the stars and planets at the time of our birth can affect our personality, behaviors, and life path.
Practice:
Birth Chart Analysis: Obtain and study your natal chart to understand the influence of celestial bodies on your life. Consult with an experienced astrologer for deeper insights.
Daily Observations: Pay attention to planetary transits and their potential effects on your mood, energy levels, and interactions.

The Role of Tarot and Divination in Self-Discovery

Tarot cards and other forms of divination can provide insights into your subconscious mind and guide your spiritual journey. These tools can help clarify your thoughts, reveal hidden patterns, and offer guidance.

Practice:

Tarot Readings: Learn to read tarot cards or seek readings from experienced practitioners. Use the insights gained for self-reflection and decision-making.

Divination Tools: Explore other divination tools such as runes, I Ching, or pendulums. Approach each method with an open mind and a willingness to learn.

Understanding and Working with Chakras and Energy Centers

Chakras are energy centers within the body that influence our physical, emotional, and spiritual well-being. There are seven main chakras, each associated with specific qualities and functions.

Practice:

Chakra Meditation: Meditate on each chakra, visualizing its color and qualities. Focus on balancing and harmonizing your energy centers.

Energy Healing: Explore practices like Reiki, acupuncture, or crystal healing to work with your energy centers. Seek guidance from experienced practitioners to deepen your understanding and practice.

QUESTIONS FOR CONTEMPLATION

What beliefs, habits, or attachments am I holding onto that may be limiting my ability to expand my consciousness?

How can I cultivate greater presence in my daily life to access deeper levels of awareness and connection?

When I experience moments of discomfort or resistance, how can I use them as opportunities for growth and transformation?

In what ways can I align my inner practices with the universal flow of life to deepen my connection to the infinite?

Notes

Part 5

COLLECTIVE AND COSMIC EVOLUTION

Chapter 26

THE COLLECTIVE SHIFT: HOW YOUR EVOLUTION CONTRIBUTES TO HUMANITY'S AWAKENING

"THE COLLECTIVE AWAKENING TO 5D CONSCIOUSNESS BEGINS WITH INDIVIDUAL HEARTS CHOOSING LOVE, UNITY, AND HIGHER PURPOSE."
– ZEN

The collective shift to 5D consciousness represents a profound transformation in human awareness and global unity. It is not just an individual journey but a shared awakening that impacts the entire planet. As more individuals begin to anchor 5D consciousness—living from the heart, embracing love, and recognizing unity—these changes ripple outward, influencing communities, societies, and eventually, the collective consciousness of humanity.

At the core of this shift is the realization that we are all interconnected. In 3D consciousness, life is often seen through the lens of separation, where individuals focus primarily on personal survival, success, and gain. The 4D phase of transition begins to break down this illusion, as people become aware of their energetic connection to others, nature, and the universe. When this awareness expands into 5D, the sense of unity becomes unmistakable. People start to understand that what they think, feel, and do impacts not only their own lives but also the lives of others. This awareness fosters greater compassion, responsibility, and a desire to contribute to the well-being of the collective.

The shift to 5D is not happening by chance; it is a necessary evolution driven by the challenges and crises facing humanity. Social, economic, and environmental upheavals have served as catalysts, urging individuals to reassess their priorities, beliefs, and values. In many ways, the breakdown of old systems has created space for new ways of thinking and being.

As people experience the limitations of fear-based living—conflict, scarcity, and control—they become more open to exploring heart-centered alternatives that promote peace, abundance, and co-creation. This willingness to explore new paradigms is the foundation of the collective shift to 5D.

One of the most visible signs of the collective awakening is the rise of movements focused on social justice, environmental sustainability, and mental well-being. These movements reflect a deeper desire for fairness, compassion, and respect for all forms of life. As individuals embody 5D consciousness, they naturally gravitate toward causes that align with their values, seeking to create positive change in their communities and beyond. This shift is not about imposing beliefs or forcing others to change; it is about leading by example —living authentically and inspiring others to do the same through personal transformation.

Communication plays a crucial role in the collective shift to 5D. In 5D consciousness, communication becomes more transparent, heart-centered, and collaborative. People are more willing to listen deeply, understand different perspectives, and find common ground. Conflict, when it arises, is seen as an opportunity for growth and understanding rather than division. This approach to communication helps dissolve fear, judgment, and competition, replacing them with empathy, trust, and cooperation. It is a powerful tool for creating harmony within relationships, communities, and societies.

The collective shift to 5D is also marked by changes in global consciousness. As more people awaken to their true nature, the collective vibration of the planet rises.

This elevation in frequency creates a tipping point, where the dominant energy becomes one of love, compassion, and unity. This shift is not just a spiritual concept but has tangible effects on the physical world, including improvements in social systems, increased cooperation among nations, and more sustainable ways of living. It is a slow but steady transformation, driven by each individual's decision to live from the heart and contribute positively to the whole.

While the collective shift to 5D brings hope and possibility, it also comes with challenges. The process of awakening can be unsettling, as it often involves facing shadow aspects, releasing attachments, and letting go of old paradigms. At the global level, this can manifest as social unrest, economic instability, or resistance to change. However, these challenges are part of the birthing process, clearing the path for a more compassionate, just, and unified world. By remaining grounded, centered, and committed to the principles of 5D living, individuals can navigate these turbulent times with grace and resilience.

As more individuals embrace 5D consciousness, the collective shift becomes not only possible but inevitable. It is a journey that requires faith, persistence, and a willingness to let go of the familiar in favor of the unknown. The collective awakening is not about perfection but about progress—moving toward a world that reflects the highest ideals of love, peace, and unity. Each act of kindness, each moment of compassion, and each effort toward unity contributes to this global transformation.

Community and Collective Awakening

The Power of Collective Consciousness and Community

Collective consciousness refers to the shared beliefs, values, and attitudes of a group. Participating in spiritual communities can amplify individual awakening and create a supportive environment for growth.

Practice:
- Group Meditation: Join or organize group meditation sessions. The combined energy can enhance the experience and foster a sense of unity.
- Spiritual Groups: Participate in spiritual groups, workshops, or retreats to connect with like-minded individuals and share experiences.

Participating in Spiritual Groups and Retreats

Spiritual groups and retreats provide opportunities for deep immersion in spiritual practices, away from the distractions of daily life. These experiences can foster profound transformation and community building.

Practice:
- Retreats: Attend spiritual retreats that focus on practices such as meditation, yoga, or mindfulness. Use these opportunities to deepen your practice and connect with others.
- Workshops: Participate in workshops and seminars on topics that interest you. Engage with the community and share your experiences and insights.

Engaging in Social and Environmental Activism

Awakening is not just an individual journey but also involves contributing to the well-being of the larger community and the planet. Engaging in social and environmental activism aligns your actions with your spiritual values.

Practice:
- Volunteer Work: Get involved in volunteer work that resonates with your values. This could include environmental conservation, social justice initiatives, or community service.
- Advocacy: Advocate for causes you believe in. Use your voice and resources to support positive change in your community and beyond.

Advanced practices for deepening consciousness involve exploring altered states, understanding the role of psychedelics, engaging in mystical and esoteric practices, and participating in community and collective awakening. These practices offer profound opportunities for personal and spiritual growth. Approach them with respect, caution, and an open heart, and allow them to guide you on your journey to deeper consciousness and awakening.

The Ripple Effect: How Your Energy Impacts the World

One of the core principles of 5D consciousness is the understanding that everything is energy. Your thoughts, emotions, and actions carry a specific energetic frequency, and this energy is not contained within you—it extends outward, influencing the people and environments around you. When you shift into a higher state of consciousness, you raise not only your own vibration but also the vibration of those around you.

This is often called the ripple effect. Imagine that you are a pebble being dropped into a still pond. The moment you touch the water, ripples begin to spread out in all directions. In the same way, when you raise your vibration through love, gratitude, and higher awareness, your energy creates ripples that touch the lives of others, whether you are aware of it or not.

Your energy can uplift the people you interact with, inspire those who observe your journey, and contribute to the collective frequency of the planet. Even small acts of kindness, moments of compassion, or positive shifts in your own mindset can have a profound impact on the world around you. The more individuals awaken to 5D consciousness, the greater the collective vibration of humanity becomes, and the faster the global shift unfolds.

The Role of Lightworkers and Way-Showers

As you evolve into 5D consciousness, you may begin to recognize yourself as a lightworker or a way-shower. Lightworkers are individuals who are here to raise the vibration of the planet through their energy, actions, and presence. Way-showers are those who lead by example, guiding others toward higher consciousness by embodying the principles of love, unity, and compassion in their own lives.

Whether you identify with these terms or not, the fact that you are on this journey means that you are contributing to the awakening of humanity. By healing yourself, raising your vibration, and living in alignment with your soul, you are creating a pathway for others to follow. You may inspire friends, family, or even strangers to begin their own journey of awakening simply by being a living example of what it means to live from the heart.

Some ways you may act as a lightworker or way-shower include:

- Holding space for others to heal, grow, or express themselves.
- Sharing your journey of awakening, whether through conversation, writing, or creative expression.
- Leading by example by living in alignment with love, peace, and unity.
- Offering compassion to those who are still operating in 3D consciousness, knowing that they are on their own unique path.

Remember, you don't have to be perfect to inspire others. Simply by doing the inner work and striving to live in alignment with 5D principles, you are contributing to the greater awakening of humanity.

The Shift from Fear to Love

The global shift into 5D consciousness is fundamentally a shift from fear to love. In 3D, fear has been the dominant frequency, creating a world based on division, conflict, and competition. People are taught to fear the unknown, to compete for resources, and to protect themselves from perceived threats. This fear-based mentality has led to the creation of systems and structures that reinforce separation and inequality.

As more people awaken to 5D consciousness, the energy of love begins to replace the energy of fear. Love is the frequency of unity, compassion, and cooperation. When you live from the frequency of love, you naturally contribute to creating a world that reflects those values. Systems of fear and control begin to break down, and new systems based on equality, collaboration, and respect for all life start to emerge.

Every time you choose love over fear in your own life—whether by forgiving someone, expressing gratitude, or trusting in the flow of life—you are adding to the collective frequency of love on the planet. This shift from fear to love is the foundation of the global awakening, and it is happening one heart at a time.

The Collective Awakening and Earth's Ascension

The collective awakening is often described as part of Earth's ascension process. This refers to the idea that not only are individuals evolving into higher states of consciousness, but the Earth itself is undergoing a transformation. Many spiritual traditions believe that the planet is moving into a higher frequency, and as it does, humanity is being called to rise to meet that frequency.

This ascension process is why so many people are experiencing awakenings at this time. As the planet's vibration increases, individuals who are attuned to this shift begin to awaken to their true nature, realizing that they are not separate from the Earth or from each other. The collective awakening is a response to this planetary ascension, and it is an essential part of humanity's evolution.

You are an integral part of this process. As you awaken, you help anchor higher frequencies of love and light on the planet, making it easier for others to do the same. The more individuals who awaken to 5D consciousness, the more the collective consciousness of humanity rises, creating a powerful force for positive change.

Creating a New Earth

One of the most exciting aspects of the collective shift is the idea of creating a New Earth. The New Earth refers to a reality in which humanity lives in harmony with nature, with each other, and with the universe. It is a world based on unity, cooperation, and love, where the old systems of fear, separation, and control have been replaced by structures that support the well-being of all life.

As you evolve into 5D consciousness, you become a co-creator of this New Earth. Your thoughts, intentions, and actions are contributing to the creation of a new reality—one that is based on the principles of love, peace, and unity. This doesn't mean abandoning the physical world; rather, it means transforming the way we live, work, and relate to each other to reflect higher consciousness.

Here are a few ways you can contribute to creating the New Earth:

- Living in alignment with 5D values: By embodying love, compassion, and unity in your daily life, you help create the foundation for the New Earth.
- Contributing to sustainable living: Supporting practices that honor the Earth, such as sustainable agriculture, renewable energy, and environmental conservation, helps create a world that is in harmony with nature.
- Spreading higher consciousness: Sharing your knowledge, experiences, and insights about 5D consciousness helps others awaken and contribute to the collective shift.

The New Earth is not a distant dream; it is being created in the present moment, by people like you who are committed to living from their highest selves and contributing to the evolution of humanity.

QUESTIONS FOR CONTEMPLATION

How do you experience your connection to the collective, and in what ways can you contribute to the global shift toward unity and compassion?

What societal issues resonate most deeply with you, and how can you take action in a way that aligns with 5D principles of love and co-creation?

Reflect on a recent conflict, either personal or global, and consider how it could be approached from a place of understanding and collaboration rather than division.

How can you communicate more transparently and empathetically, both in your personal relationships and in the wider community?

In what ways can you anchor 5D consciousness in your daily life, knowing that your choices contribute to the collective vibration of the planet?

Notes

chapter 27

LIVING IN ALIGNMENT: CONTINUING THE JOURNEY OF EVOLUTION

"WHEN YOU LIVE IN ALIGNMENT WITH YOUR TRUE SELF, LIFE FLOWS EFFORTLESSLY, GUIDED BY PURPOSE AND AUTHENTICITY."
– ZEN

Living in alignment is about synchronizing your inner world with your outer actions. It involves consistently making choices that reflect your core values, soul's purpose, and true essence. This state of alignment brings a sense of peace, flow, and fulfillment, as life unfolds naturally and effortlessly when you are attuned to your higher self. In contrast, living out of alignment often results in feelings of discontent, anxiety, and resistance, as actions are driven by fear, obligation, or external expectations rather than inner guidance. Alignment starts with self-awareness. To live in alignment, you must first have a clear understanding of your values, desires, and purpose. It requires tuning in to your inner voice and trusting your intuition, even when it contradicts societal norms or the expectations of others. This process involves taking time for self-reflection, meditation, and contemplation to gain clarity about what truly matters to you. It is not always easy, as it may involve making difficult decisions, setting boundaries, or even changing directions in life. However, the rewards of living in alignment—greater peace, joy, and authenticity—make it worthwhile.

At the heart of living in alignment is the concept of integrity. Integrity means being true to yourself in all situations, honoring your commitments, and acting in ways that align with your values. This level of honesty requires vulnerability, as it involves showing up authentically, even when it feels uncomfortable.

For example, you might need to express your true feelings in a relationship, pursue a career that aligns with your passions rather than societal expectations, or say no to obligations that don't resonate with your spirit. By doing so, you create a sense of inner harmony, as your actions reflect your true self rather than a persona created to gain approval or avoid conflict.

Living in alignment also requires the ability to tune into and trust your intuition. Intuition is the voice of your higher self, guiding you toward actions and decisions that are in line with your soul's path. It often appears as a gut feeling, a sense of knowing, or a gentle nudge in a certain direction. While the rational mind may question intuitive guidance, living in alignment means giving it space and trust. This may involve making decisions that don't seem logical or practical from a 3D perspective but feel right at a deeper level. Trusting your intuition can be challenging, especially when faced with uncertainty or pressure from others, but it is a crucial component of living authentically.

Creating alignment in daily life involves conscious choices that nurture your body, mind, and spirit. It means prioritizing self-care, setting healthy boundaries, and engaging in activities that bring joy and fulfillment. For example, you might choose to spend more time in nature, engage in creative pursuits, or practice mindfulness to stay connected to your inner self. Physical alignment also matters, as the body's well-being is closely linked to mental and spiritual health. Practices like yoga, breathwork, and regular exercise help maintain balance and vitality, supporting the overall state of alignment.

Living in alignment is not about perfection but about presence. It's a dynamic process that requires continuous self-awareness and adjustment. As you evolve, your values, desires, and purpose may shift, and living in alignment means adapting to these changes with grace. It is a journey of constant refinement, where each decision, interaction, and experience offers an opportunity to deepen your connection to your true self. By living in alignment, you become a clearer channel for your higher self, allowing its wisdom, love, and guidance to flow through you more easily.

Purpose and Passion

Discovering Your Life Purpose
Discovering your life purpose involves exploring your passions, values, and strengths. It requires introspection and a willingness to follow your inner guidance.
Practice: Reflect on what brings you joy and fulfillment. Consider your talents and how you can use them to make a positive impact. Engage in activities that align with your values and passions.
Aligning Your Career with Your Values and Passions
Aligning your career with your values and passions creates a sense of meaning and fulfillment. It allows you to contribute to the world in a way that resonates with your true self.
Practice: Evaluate your current career and how it aligns with your values and passions. If necessary, consider making changes to pursue work that is more meaningful to you. Seek opportunities that allow you to use your strengths and make a positive impact.

Setting and Achieving Meaningful Goals
Setting meaningful goals provides direction and motivation. Achieving these goals requires commitment, perseverance, and a clear plan.
Practice: Set SMART goals (Specific, Measurable, Achievable, Relevant, Time-bound) that align with your values and passions. Break down larger goals into smaller, manageable steps. Regularly review your progress and adjust your plans as needed. Celebrate your achievements and learn from any setbacks.

Conscious living and lifestyle choices play a crucial role in our journey toward personal growth and spiritual awakening. By embracing sustainable living, cultivating mindful and compassionate relationships, discovering and aligning with our life purpose, and managing our time mindfully, we create a balanced and fulfilling life. These practices support our overall well-being and help us live in harmony with ourselves, others, and the planet. Embrace these principles with an open heart and mind, and allow them to guide you on your journey to conscious living.

TIP: Do Gratitude Affirmations Daily, Speak them aloud or write them down to set a positive tone for the day

QUESTIONS FOR CONTEMPLATION

Reflect on a recent decision you made. Was it in alignment with your values, or was it influenced by fear, obligation, or the expectations of others?

What core values guide your life, and how can you ensure that your daily actions reflect these values more consistently?

How do you experience intuition, and how can you strengthen your trust in this inner guidance?

In what areas of your life do you feel out of alignment, and what changes can you make to bring yourself back into harmony?

What self-care practices support your alignment with your higher self, and how can you incorporate them into your daily routine?

NOTES

chapter 28

Unity of One Consciousness: Embracing Interconnectedness

"IN THE ONENESS OF CONSCIOUSNESS, WE REMEMBER THAT SEPARATION IS AN ILLUSION AND LOVE IS OUR TRUE NATURE."
– ZEN

The concept of unity of one consciousness represents the ultimate realization of spiritual awakening. It is the understanding that, beneath the apparent differences and diversity in the world, there is a fundamental oneness that connects all beings, energies, and forms of life. This awareness transcends the limitations of the ego and dissolves the illusion of separation, revealing that everything is interconnected and part of a greater whole. Unity consciousness is not just a spiritual philosophy but a lived experience that transforms how individuals relate to themselves, others, and the universe.

At its core, unity consciousness is rooted in the idea that everything is made up of the same fundamental energy. Whether seen through the lens of quantum physics, which describes matter as interconnected waves of energy, or through spiritual traditions, which speak of a universal source, the message is the same: separation is an illusion. The perceived differences in race, religion, culture, or identity are temporary manifestations within a single, unified field of consciousness. When individuals awaken to this truth, they begin to see the world not as a collection of separate parts but as an intricate web of interconnected energies.

This realization of oneness has profound implications for personal growth and spiritual evolution. When individuals understand that they are not separate from others, it fosters a deep sense of compassion, empathy, and love. Judgments, resentments, and conflicts that arise from perceived differences start to dissolve, replaced by an understanding that all beings are simply different expressions of the same universal essence. This shift in perception creates a more harmonious relationship with oneself and others, as love, rather than fear, becomes the guiding force in interactions.

Unity consciousness also shifts how individuals perceive challenges, conflicts, and suffering. Instead of viewing problems as isolated events or blaming others, individuals begin to see challenges as collective experiences that reflect broader patterns of consciousness. For example, personal struggles may be understood as part of the collective healing process, where individual growth contributes to the evolution of the whole. This perspective not only promotes personal responsibility but also encourages collaboration, as individuals recognize that healing themselves aids in healing the collective.

Meditation and spiritual practices play a crucial role in experiencing unity consciousness. Meditation helps quiet the mind's constant chatter and dissolves the barriers created by the ego, allowing for a direct experience of oneness. During deep states of meditation, individuals often feel a sense of boundless love, peace, and interconnectedness, as if they are merging with a greater whole. This experience is often described as "losing oneself" but actually represents finding the true essence that is connected to all that is. Practices like loving-kindness meditation, which involves sending love and compassion to oneself, loved ones, and even perceived enemies, help cultivate the energy of unity in daily life.

The concept of universal love is central to unity consciousness. Universal love goes beyond romantic or familial love, extending to all beings, regardless of differences or personal connections. It is the recognition that the same divine essence exists within every living being, and that to love another is to love oneself. This type of love is unconditional, free from judgment or attachment, and promotes healing and harmony on both a personal and collective level. Practicing universal love involves actively seeking to understand, empathize with, and support others, even in challenging situations. Synchronicity is often seen as a sign of alignment with unity consciousness. As individuals raise their vibration and align with the energy of oneness, they begin to notice synchronicities—meaningful coincidences that seem to occur with a sense of divine timing. These synchronicities are not random but reflect the interconnected nature of reality, offering guidance, confirmation, or encouragement along the spiritual path. For example, meeting someone who shares similar intentions or finding information that answers a pressing question may be seen as a reflection of alignment with the greater whole.

The concept of collective consciousness also aligns with unity consciousness. Collective consciousness refers to the shared beliefs, values, and energies of a group, society, or humanity as a whole. As individuals awaken to their true nature and embody higher states of love, compassion, and unity, they contribute to raising the collective consciousness. This collective shift is not just about personal enlightenment but about creating a world that reflects the ideals of oneness, peace, and harmony. Acts of kindness, compassion, and service become ways to express unity consciousness, creating a ripple effect that influences the wider collective. Experiencing unity consciousness also involves recognizing the sacredness of all life. Whether it is the trees, animals, oceans, or stars, everything is seen as a manifestation of the same universal energy. This awareness fosters a sense of reverence and gratitude, promoting environmental stewardship and a desire to protect and nurture all forms of life. It encourages sustainable living, as individuals recognize that harm to the planet is ultimately harm to themselves and the collective.

Integration of unity consciousness into daily life is a continuous journey. It involves practicing presence, compassion, and non-judgment in every interaction, whether with loved ones, strangers, or even oneself. It is a call to live from the heart, where the energy of love flows naturally, creating a sense of peace and fulfillment that is not dependent on external circumstances. Unity consciousness is not a destination but a way of being that evolves with each moment of awareness, choice, and connection.

QUESTIONS FOR CONTEMPLATION

How do you experience the illusion of separation in your daily life, and what practices help you remember your connection to the whole?

In what ways can you cultivate universal love, extending compassion and empathy to all beings, even in challenging situations?

Have you noticed synchronicities that reflect alignment with unity consciousness? What messages or guidance have they offered?

How does understanding the concept of collective consciousness influence your approach to personal growth, relationships, or social issues?

What practices, such as meditation or acts of kindness, can help you embody unity consciousness more fully in your everyday life?

Notes

chapter 29

INVOLUTION - TURNING INWARD

"THE JOURNEY INWARD REVEALS THE UNIVERSE WITHIN, WHERE STILLNESS UNVEILS THE ESSENCE OF WHO WE TRULY ARE."
– ZEN

Involution, often described as the process of turning inward, is a crucial aspect of awakening consciousness. While evolution involves growth and expansion in the external world, involution is about exploring the inner dimensions of the self. It is the inward journey toward deeper self-awareness, spiritual understanding, and the realization of one's true essence. Involution invites you to examine your thoughts, beliefs, emotions, and experiences with curiosity and compassion, uncovering the layers of conditioning that obscure your authentic self.

The concept of involution emphasizes that spiritual growth is not just about acquiring new knowledge or achieving external goals, but about remembering who you truly are. This process involves unlearning, letting go of false identities, and shedding limiting beliefs that have been adopted through societal conditioning, upbringing, or personal trauma. By turning inward, you access the deeper wisdom of the soul, discovering the inherent peace, love, and oneness that reside within. Meditation is one of the most powerful practices for involution. It provides a quiet, sacred space for observing the mind without judgment, allowing deeper layers of consciousness to emerge. Meditation helps you become aware of the constant stream of thoughts and mental patterns that often go unnoticed but significantly shape your reality. Through regular meditation, you learn to detach from these thoughts, realizing that you are not the mind but the observer of the mind. This realization creates a sense of inner freedom, as you become less reactive and more present in each moment. Self-reflection is another essential tool for involution. It involves taking time to explore your inner landscape—your beliefs, emotions, and motivations. Journaling is a practical way to engage in self-reflection, as it allows you to put thoughts and feelings into words, bringing unconscious material to the surface. Questions like, "What do I truly want?" or "What fears are holding me back?" can help uncover deeper truths about your desires, wounds, and aspirations. By engaging in honest self-reflection, you create a pathway for deeper self-awareness and personal transformation.

Involution also requires facing the shadow aspects of the self—those parts that have been repressed, denied, or hidden due to fear or shame. This inner work involves bringing the shadow to light, understanding its origins, and integrating it with compassion. As you turn inward, you may encounter unresolved emotions, limiting beliefs, or past traumas that have been buried in the subconscious. Rather than resisting these aspects, involution encourages you to embrace them as part of your wholeness. This acceptance promotes healing, self-love, and a deeper connection to your authentic self.

Inner child work is another facet of involution, as it involves reconnecting with the younger, wounded parts of yourself that still influence adult behavior. The inner child represents both the innocence and the pain of childhood, carrying unmet needs, unhealed wounds, and unfulfilled desires. By turning inward and nurturing the inner child, you can heal past wounds, reclaim lost joy, and cultivate a stronger sense of self-worth. Inner child work often involves visualization, dialogue, and affirmations that provide love, safety, and reassurance to this vulnerable part of yourself.

Involution is not just about addressing wounds or past experiences; it is also about connecting with the higher self—the aspect of you that is aligned with universal consciousness. The higher self is the inner guide that offers wisdom, intuition, and clarity, supporting you in making decisions that resonate with your soul's purpose. Connecting with the higher self can be facilitated through meditation, prayer, or simply tuning into your inner voice during moments of stillness. This connection helps you access a deeper sense of peace, purpose, and alignment, allowing you to navigate life with greater ease and trust.

One of the core principles of involution is self-acceptance. True spiritual growth requires acknowledging and embracing all aspects of the self, including the flaws, fears, and imperfections. This acceptance creates a foundation of unconditional love, where you no longer seek validation or approval from external sources but find wholeness within. Self-acceptance also fosters greater compassion for others, as you recognize that everyone is on their own journey of involution, facing their own shadows, wounds, and inner struggles.

Involution also emphasizes the importance of presence. By turning inward, you become more aware of the present moment, experiencing life directly rather than through the filters of past conditioning or future expectations. Presence involves being fully engaged with what is happening now, whether it's a conversation, a feeling, or a simple observation. It helps quiet the mind's chatter, creating space for the inner voice of wisdom to emerge. Practicing mindfulness, whether through formal meditation or mindful awareness in daily life, supports the process of involution by bringing attention back to the here and now.

The journey of involution ultimately leads to a deeper realization of oneness. As you turn inward and peel away the layers of conditioning, you discover that the separation between the self and others is an illusion. You come to understand that the essence of who you are is connected to the essence of all life. This awareness fosters a sense of unity, compassion, and love for all beings, as you recognize that the inner journey is a microcosm of the collective journey of awakening consciousness.

Affirmations for Involution

"I embrace the stillness within, knowing that all the answers I seek reside in my soul."

"With each moment of introspection, I uncover deeper truths about my essence and purpose."

"I trust the inward journey to guide me toward alignment, healing, and self-awareness."

QUESTIONS FOR CONTEMPLATION

What beliefs or patterns have you recently uncovered through turning inward, and how have they shaped your current reality?

How can you create more time and space in your daily life for meditation, self-reflection, or inner child work?

In what ways do you resist certain aspects of yourself, and how can you cultivate greater self-acceptance and compassion?

How does connecting with your higher self influence your decision-making, relationships, or sense of purpose?

How can practicing presence, whether through meditation or mindful awareness, support your journey of involution and inner peace?

Notes

Conclusion: Embracing the Journey of Awakening

The journey of awakening consciousness is both profound and deeply personal. It is not a linear path but a spiral of growth, where each insight, challenge, and transformation builds upon the last. This process requires courage, commitment, and a willingness to explore the depths of the self, embracing both light and shadow. It invites you to peel back the layers of conditioning, heal old wounds, and align more deeply with your true essence.

Awakening is not about reaching a state of perfection or achieving a final destination; it is about continuous evolution, where each moment becomes an opportunity for greater awareness, love, and unity. It is about cultivating presence, connecting with the higher self, and living from the heart. This journey encompasses the integration of past experiences, the balance of inner energies, and the realization of oneness with all life.

The topics explored throughout this book—energy healing, shadow integration, manifesting, quantum consciousness, and more—are tools and concepts to guide you along this path. While each chapter offers insights and practices, remember that awakening is ultimately an experiential process. It is about applying what you learn, observing how it impacts your life, and adapting as you grow. Spiritual growth is not always easy, but it is always rewarding, as it leads to greater peace, joy, and fulfillment.

As you continue to awaken, know that you are not alone.

Countless others are on this journey, each contributing to the collective shift toward higher consciousness. Together, you are creating a world that reflects love, compassion, and unity—values that are not just ideals but lived realities. The world you wish to see begins within you, and by embodying your highest self, you become a beacon of light for others.

Embrace this journey with an open heart, knowing that each step, no matter how small, is a step toward your awakening. Trust in the process, honor your experiences, and always remember that your essence is love, peace, and unity. Your journey is your gift to the world, and it is through your awakening that the collective consciousness evolves.

Compassion and Gratitude

Compassion and gratitude are powerful forces that can transform your journey. Compassion for yourself and others fosters a loving and supportive environment for growth. It encourages you to approach challenges with kindness and understanding, rather than judgment. Gratitude, on the other hand, shifts your focus from what is lacking to what is abundant in your life. By regularly practicing gratitude, you cultivate a positive mindset that attracts more joy, peace, and fulfillment. Take time each day to reflect on what you are grateful for, and express this gratitude through your actions and words.

Trusting the Process

Awakening is a deeply personal and often unpredictable process. It requires trust—trust in yourself, in the practices you engage in, and in the journey itself. There will be moments of clarity and moments of confusion, times of great insight and times of seeming stagnation. Each phase of the journey is valuable and necessary for your growth. Trust that you are exactly where you need to be at this moment. Even when the path seems unclear, know that every experience, every challenge, and every triumph is part of your evolution. Embrace each moment with an open heart and a willing spirit, and allow the process to unfold naturally.

Moving Forward

As you close this book, you open a new chapter in your journey of awakening. Take with you the insights, practices, and wisdom shared within these pages. Let them serve as a guide and a companion as you continue to explore the depths of your consciousness and the heights of your potential. Remember, awakening is not about becoming someone new but about becoming who you truly are. It is about shedding the layers of conditioning, fear, and limitation to reveal the radiant being within. Embrace your journey with courage, compassion, and curiosity. Allow yourself to be transformed by the process and trust that each step you take brings you closer to your true essence.

Thank you for embarking on this journey with me. May your path be filled with light, love, and profound awakening. Trust in your journey, embrace your unique essence, and let your consciousness evolve into its highest expression.

- **You are a creator, a healer, and an integral part of the universal whole.**
- **Every thought, action, and intention contributes to the greater shift toward unity consciousness.**
- **Trust yourself, follow your heart, and allow the universe to guide you on your path.**
- **Remember: the journey of awakening is not about becoming something new but about remembering who you truly are.**

"AWAKENING IS NOT A DESTINATION BUT A RETURN TO YOUR TRUEST SELF"
-ZEN

FINAL THOUGHTS

"Awaken Your Consciousness" is not just a book but a call to action—a call to live more mindfully, love more deeply, and connect more authentically with yourself and the world around you. As you continue on this path, know that you are part of a larger movement of awakening, one that is transforming the world, one conscious soul at a time.

May you find peace in the present moment, strength in your journey, and joy in the unfolding of your true self. Embrace the adventure of awakening, and let your light shine brightly. The world needs your unique essence, and your journey is a gift to all.

With deep gratitude, love and unwavering support,

K. Martin

Check Out Our Pages

Visit our store:
stan.store/essenceevolution28

Socials

TIKTOK.COM/@ESSENCEEVOLUTION28

YOUTUBE.COM/@ESSENCEEVOLUTION28

INSTAGRAM.COM/ESSENCEEVOLUTION28

FACEBOOK:.COM/@ESSENCE.EVOLUTION.28

Manufactured by Amazon.ca
Acheson, AB

15313313R00140